RAND NATIONAL DEFENSE RESEARCH INSTITUTE

Evaluating the Implementation of the Re-Engineering Systems of Primary Care Treatment in the Military (RESPECT-Mil)

Eunice C. Wong, Lisa H. Jaycox, Lynsay Ayer, Caroline Epley, Racine Harris, Scott Naftel, Susan M. Paddock

Prepared for the Office of the Secretary of Defense

For more information on this publication, visit www.rand.org/t/RR588

Library of Congress Cataloging-in-Publication Data is available for this publication.

ISBN: 978-0-8330-8898-7

Published by the RAND Corporation, Santa Monica, Calif.

© Copyright 2015 RAND Corporation

RAND® is a registered trademark.

Support RAND

Make a tax-deductible charitable contribution at
www.rand.org/giving/contribute

www.rand.org

Preface

During the decade following the September 11, 2001, terrorist attacks, approximately 2.6 million U.S. service members were deployed to support combat operations in Afghanistan (Operation Enduring Freedom) and Iraq (Operations Iraqi Freedom and New Dawn) (U.S. Government Accountability Office [GAO], 2011). The U.S. military has been functioning at an unprecedented high operational tempo, as evidenced by the multiple deployments of more than a third of these U.S. service members and the extended period of conflict (GAO, 2011). The psychological toll of these protracted combat operations on U.S. service members has garnered increasing concern. The Department of Defense (DoD) has engaged in a series of efforts to ensure that the military health system is adequately positioned to address the psychological health needs of service members.

In 2009, the Defense Centers of Excellence for Psychological Health and Traumatic Brain Injury (DCoE) requested the RAND Corporation's assistance in assessing the effectiveness of DoD-sponsored programs aimed at promoting the psychological health of service members and their families. One of the programs selected for evaluation is the Re-Engineering Systems of Primary Care Treatment in the Military (RESPECT-Mil), a system of care designed to screen, assess, and treat posttraumatic stress disorder and depression among active duty service members in the Army's primary care settings.

This report details RAND's independent evaluation of the implementation of RESPECT-Mil. Analyses were based on existing program data used to monitor fidelity to RESPECT-Mil across the Army's primary care clinics, as well as discussions with key stakeholders.

This report will be of particular interest to policymakers and officials within the DoD who are responsible for developing and implementing programs to address the psychological health of service members, especially within the context of military primary care settings.

This research was sponsored by the Assistant Secretary of Defense for Health Affairs and the DCoE and conducted within the Forces and Resources Policy Center of the RAND National Defense Research Institute, a federally funded research and development center sponsored by the Office of the Secretary of Defense, the Joint Staff, the Unified Combatant Commands, the Navy, the Marine Corps, the defense agencies, and the defense Intelligence Community. This report is one of a series of program evaluations conducted as part of the Innovative Practices for Psychological Health and Traumatic Brain Injury project; for more information and to access other products from this project, please visit the project web page (http://www.rand.org/multi/military/innovative-practices.html).

For more information on the RAND Forces and Resources Policy Center, see http://www.rand.org/nsrd/ndri/centers/frp.html or contact the director (contact information is provided on the web page).

Contents

Figures and Tables

Figures

Tables

Summary

The Re-Engineering Systems of Primary Care Treatment in the Military (RESPECT-Mil) Program is a system of care designed to screen, assess, and treat posttraumatic stress disorder (PTSD) and depression among active duty service members in the Army's primary care settings. A team of researchers from RAND evaluated the implementation of the program in military treatment facilities based on existing program data and discussions with key stakeholders. This report presents results from the evaluation and makes recommendations intended to improve the implementation of collaborative care models such as RESPECT-Mil in military treatment settings. Lessons learned may apply to other primary care–based models that facilitate and coordinate care for behavioral health needs (e.g., Patient Centered Medical Home, or PCMH).

Background

Improving Access to Mental Health Services for Active Duty Service Members

Despite high rates of need, many service members do not seek mental health care. Among active duty service members with probable PTSD or depression, nearly half have not sought any mental health care in the prior year (Schell and Marshall, 2008). The Department of Defense (DoD) Task Force on Mental Health put forth a recommendation to embed mental health professionals in primary care settings as one way to increase the accessibility of mental health services among service members (Department of Defense Task Force on Mental Health, 2007). This recommendation is based on the view that primary care settings may be less stigmatizing than specialty mental health clinics. Identifying service members with unmet mental health needs in primary care and connecting them to services in the same setting may be an effective means for increasing access to treatment. Service members make an average of three primary care visits per year; women and those with PTSD access primary care at even higher rates (Frayne et al., 2011).

Effective approaches to integrating mental health treatment within primary care have been established for depression and anxiety in civilian settings (Archer et al., 2012; Thota et al., 2012). Similar efforts have been under way in the Department of Veterans Affairs (VA) for several years now but have mostly targeted depression (Felker et al., 2006; Fortney, Enderle, et al., 2012). DoD has launched programs to integrate mental health care into military primary care settings with active duty service members, but these programs have not been evaluated extensively (Weinick et al., 2011).

In 2009, the Defense Centers of Excellence for Psychological Health and Traumatic Brain Injury (DCoE) asked RAND to evaluate DoD-sponsored programs aimed at promoting the psychological health of service members and their families. One of the programs selected for evaluation was RESPECT-Mil.

Origins and Components of the RESPECT-Mil Program

RESPECT-Mil is based on a collaborative care model known as Re-Engineering Primary Care Treatment of Depression (RESPECT-D) (Dietrich et al., 2004). At the center of RESPECT-D is its Three Component Model (3CM), a systematic integrated team approach to depression care involving three core components: (1) the primary care clinician and practice, (2) care management, and (3) a collaborating mental health specialist. RESPECT-D was designed to account for challenges in implementing and sustaining collaborative care programs in real-world settings that lack intensive, externally funded research support. RESPECT-D is composed of practical, evidence-based clinical routines for depression management intended to facilitate broad dissemination using available resources within health care organizations. RESPECT-D has been found to substantially improve depression-related outcomes and treatment satisfaction compared with treatment as usual in primary care (Dietrich et al., 2004). RESPECT-Mil builds on RESPECT-D by using the 3CM to improve the management of PTSD and depression in the Army's primary care clinics.

Analogous to RESPECT-D, RESPECT-Mil has three components: (1) the primary care provider and prepared practice, (2) the RESPECT-Mil care facilitator, and (3) the behavioral health specialist, more commonly referred to as the *behavioral health champion* (Engel et al., 2008). The primary care provider and prepared practice provide routine screening, assessment, and management of PTSD and depression. The primary care provider works with service members to develop a treatment plan, which may include psychotropic medication, counseling, and self-management strategies. The care facilitator plays a supportive role by promoting service members' adherence to treatment plans. Care facilitators achieve this via monthly follow-up contacts during which they attend to service member needs, monitor treatment adherence and response, and encourage self-management strategies. Care facilitators keep the primary care provider and the behavioral health champion abreast of the service members' treatment experiences. The behavioral health champion, typically a psychiatrist, provides clinical and pharmacotherapy advice to the primary care provider, monitors service members' treatment progress with the care facilitator, and facilitates referrals to specialty care when indicated.

In addition to the 3CM, the U.S. Army Medical Command ordered the formation of the RESPECT-Mil Implementation Team to provide program management, training, oversight, and assistance to Army installations assigned to implement RESPECT-Mil (U.S. Army Medical Command Operation Order 07-34; see U.S. Army Medical Command, 2007).[1] Beginning in 2007, the program was implemented at 15 Army military treatment facilities, involving 43 primary care clinics. By the summer of 2012, RESPECT-Mil had expanded to 37 Army installations and more than 90 clinics (Deployment Health Clinical Center, 2012). RESPECT-Mil represents one of the largest undertakings to implement collaborative care for PTSD and depression in real-world settings.

---

[1]   Though formed in response to the U.S. Army Medical Command Operation Order 07-34, the RESPECT-Mil Implementation Team was not actually within the Army chain of command.

RAND's Evaluation Goals

RAND's evaluation focused on the implementation of RESPECT-Mil. The evaluation had three specific aims: (1) assess the degree to which RESPECT-Mil is being implemented in the Army's primary care settings; (2) identify facilitators and barriers to implementation; and (3) examine the sustainability of RESPECT-Mil according to the perspectives of key stakeholders in the military health system. We map these three aims onto the Reach, Efficacy, Adoption, Implementation, Maintenance (RE-AIM) framework (Glasgow, Vogt, and Boles, 1999). The RE-AIM framework has been used as a model for evaluating the implementation or translation of evidence-based practices into real-world settings (Meyer et al., 2012; Rogers et al., 2013).

According to the RE-AIM framework, the implementation and public health impact of an evidence-based intervention depends on the following factors: the scope and extent to which the intervention *reaches* the targeted population; the *efficacy* of the intervention in yielding positive outcomes; the degree of *adoption* of the intervention across a substantial proportion of settings; the level of *implementation* fidelity with respect to whether the intervention is being delivered as designed; and the viability of the long-term *maintenance* of the intervention.

For aim 1, we examined the implementation of RESPECT-Mil in relation to the *reach, adoption, implementation* fidelity, and *efficacy* of the program.[2] Aims 2 and 3 explore factors associated with the *maintenance* of collaborative care programs like RESPECT-Mil. Aim 2 identifies facilitators and barriers to implementing RESPECT-Mil from the perspective of providers and the RESPECT-Mil Implementation Team. Aim 3 assesses the sustainability of the program from the vantage point of stakeholders in the military health system.

Methodological Approach

For aim 1, we relied on two data sources that the RESPECT-Mil Implementation Team maintains for the purposes of program oversight—Monthly Screening and Referral Clinic Reports and the Fast Informative Risk and Safety Tracker and Stepped Treatment Entry and Planning System (FIRST-STEPS). Data were extracted from these two sources for the period of August 2011 to March 2012 for 37 U.S. Army installations with 84 primary care clinics. The Monthly Screening and Referral Clinic Reports track screening and referral practices for PTSD and depression. FIRST-STEPS is an electronic case-management tracking tool designed for use by care facilitators and behavioral health champions. FIRST-STEPS contains records on care facilitator contacts, clinical assessments, medication and counseling adherence, engagement in psychoeducation and self-management goals, and final dispositions of case closures.[3]

For aim 2, we spoke with RESPECT-Mil providers and the RESPECT-Mil Implementation Team to identify facilitators and barriers to implementation. A total of 35 RESPECT-Mil

---

[2] The efficacy of an intervention can be tested using a variety of study designs. A randomized controlled trial in which PTSD and depression outcomes are compared among service members who are randomly assigned to RESPECT-Mil or usual care is considered the most rigorous test of efficacy. However, this was not possible given that the program had already been implemented throughout most of the Army installations before the start of the evaluation. This evaluation naturalistically investigated changes in clinical symptoms and functioning to examine the impact of the program on participants.

[3] The RESPECT-Mil Implementation Team has not had access to the kind of data obtained for the current evaluation (i.e., aggregated individual-level data over the entire course of treatment). This has precluded a more fine-grained assessment of the implementation of RESPECT-Mil, which is provided in the current report.

providers participated in the study (i.e., 11 care facilitators, seven behavioral health champions, eight primary care champions, and nine primary care providers), while all 11 of the RESPECT-Mil Implementation Team members participated (e.g., program director, deputy director, behavioral health and care facilitator proponent, program evaluators, database managers and analysts, and administrative assistants). For aim 3, we relied on discussions with key stakeholders within the military health system and with the RESPECT-Mil Implementation Team to gain further insight to factors that may influence the sustainability of the program. Personnel from the Regional Medical Commands, U.S. Army Medical Department, U.S. Army Medical Commands, the Office of the Assistant Secretary of Defense for Health Affairs, and Tricare Management Activity were invited to take part in the study. A total of 24 of 43 key stakeholders who were contacted agreed to participate.

Findings

Aim 1: Extent of Implementation of RESPECT-Mil in Army Primary Care Settings
Reach

To determine the reach of RESPECT-Mil, we asked the following question: *To what extent does RESPECT-Mil facilitate the identification of service members with mental health needs related to depression and/or PTSD?*

- Of the primary care visits made from August 2011 to March 2012, 93 percent (599,760) included screens for PTSD and depression.
- Of the screened visits, 13 percent (77,998) resulted in a positive screen.
- Of the positive screens, 61 percent (47,797) resulted in a probable diagnosis of a mental health disorder:
    – Forty-six percent (36,231) of positive screens had a diagnosis of PTSD, depression, or both.
    – Fifteen percent (11,566) of positive screens had a diagnosis other than PTSD or depression.

Of the approximately 80,000 positive screens, a breakdown of their final disposition is as follows (final dispositions of the remaining 2 percent [1,617] were unknown due to missing data):[4]

- Sixteen percent (12,835) resulted in a referral being accepted to one or more of the following sources of care: enhanced primary care treatment (i.e., RESPECT-Mil), behavioral health, or another psychosocial resource.
- Eight percent (6,353) resulted in a referral being declined to RESPECT-Mil, behavioral health, or both.
- Five percent (4,033) resulted in the need being addressed in primary care "as usual."
- Thirteen percent (10,172) resulted in no behavioral health need being identified.
- Fifty-five percent (42,988) were recorded as already being in one or more sources of mental health treatment.

---

[4] The Monthly Screening and Referral Clinic Reports track the final disposition of only positive screens. The final disposition of visits in which a probable diagnosis is identified is not tracked and thus is not provided in this report.

Findings indicate that at an absolute level, RESPECT-Mil is identifying a considerable number of service members who are reporting depression and PTSD symptoms, as evidenced by the number of positive screens resulting from routine screening. Moreover, a substantial proportion of positive screens are resulting in the detection of probable diagnoses of depression and PTSD and other mental diagnoses. Of the total positive screens, only a smaller proportion (13 percent) had no behavioral health need identified. Of the 19,188 referrals provided (referrals accepted plus referrals declined), approximately two-thirds were accepted, resulting in a sizeable number of service members being connected to needed mental health care. More than half of the positive screens were composed of service members who were already in treatment but were still symptomatic. To the extent that routine screenings can facilitate additional support for service members who are engaged in treatment but are not progressing sufficiently, this may be another venue in which RESPECT-Mil can address unmet mental health needs.

Adoption

To examine the level of *adoption* of RESPECT-Mil,[5] we analyzed the screening and referral rates for each of the 37 Army installations that had implemented RESPECT-Mil. This helped answer the following question: *How do Army installations vary with respect to the identification and referral of service members with mental health needs?*

- A majority of installations (25 out of 37) were screening a high proportion of visits (ranging from 91 to 99 percent); 31 of 37 installations were screening at least 80 percent of their visits.
- In many cases, service members who screened positive were already in treatment. At 20 of the 37 installations, 50 percent or more of those screening positive were recorded as already receiving care.
- For ten of the 37 installations, at least 20 percent of positive screens resulted in an accepted referral to RESPECT-Mil; 24 of the installations had rates between 10 percent and 19 percent.
- Of positive screens, five of the 37 installations had rates of declined referrals to RESPECT-Mil that were 10 percent or higher.

Most installations were conducting depression and PTSD screening for a large proportion of primary care visits. Rates of positive screens were also fairly uniform across sites. In contrast, rates of probable diagnosis resulting from positive screens were more variable, with no evident or consistent relationship to length of implementation time. With respect to rates of referrals of positive screens, variation also occurred across sites but with no clear relationship to length of implementation time. Thus, implementing RESPECT-Mil over a longer duration does not guarantee greater rates of identification and referral of service members with mental health needs. Further, the extent to which variations in probable diagnoses and referral rates are due to service member factors (e.g., differences in clinical symptoms, willingness to disclose, or preferences for certain types of services is unknown) versus provider factors (e.g., administration of clinical assessments, willingness to address mental health needs) is unknown.

---

[5] Adoption indicators could only be derived from screening and referral clinic data because they contained installation site information. Adoption indicators could not be derived for other RESPECT-Mil components (e.g., care facilitator contacts) because FIRST-STEPS data do not contain installation site information.

Implementation Fidelity

The RAND team analyzed data from FIRST-STEPS, an electronic case-management tracking tool, to examine the implementation of key components of RESPECT-Mil. We extracted clinical assessment and treatment monitoring information for 3,043 service members who were enrolled in RESPECT-Mil during the period between August 2011 and March 2012. Below are the main findings to the questions we posed regarding the implementation fidelity of RESPECT-Mil. We asked: *To what degree is RESPECT-Mil enrolling service members with depression and/or PTSD?*

Of the 3,403 service members enrolled in RESPECT-Mil:

- Sixteen percent (549) had no symptoms or minimal symptoms.
- Another 14 percent (473) were missing clinical assessments at baseline.
- The remaining 70 percent (2,381) were classified according to one of the baseline clinical status categories created for this study (i.e., depression prominent, PTSD prominent, depression plus PTSD prominent). Of the 3,403 service members enrolled in RESPECT-Mil:
    - Twenty-one percent (716) were classified as "depression prominent" (mild to severe depression).
    - Twenty-six percent (875) were classified as "PTSD prominent" (mild to severe PTSD).
    - Twenty-three percent (790) were classified as "depression + PTSD prominent" (mild to severe depression and PTSD).

RESPECT-Mil enrolled, at somewhat comparable rates, service members with depression prominent, PTSD prominent, and depression plus PTSD prominent symptoms. Enrolled service members also exhibited a wide range of clinical symptom severity levels. A proportion of service members are also presenting with no or minimal depression and/or PTSD symptoms.

We also asked: *To what extent are care facilitators able to implement their RESPECT-Mil responsibilities?* To facilitate comparisons between our findings and other collaborative care studies, we focused on the 2,381 service members who had mild to severe depression and/or PTSD symptoms (i.e., service members classified with one of the baseline clinical status categories). These are the main findings regarding care facilitator contacts:

- Of the 2,381 service members who were classified with one of the baseline clinical status categories:
    - Thirty-eight percent (897) had their cases closed after the initial primary care referral to RESPECT-Mil and had no contacts with the care facilitator. This proportion is in the middle range compared with similar studies of collaborative care programs (e.g., Wells, Sherbourne, Schoenbaum, et al., 2000; Chaney et al., 2011).
    - Twenty-three percent (541) only had an initial care facilitator contact.
    - Thirty-nine percent (943) had an initial care facilitator contact and at least one monthly follow-up contact. This rate of follow-up contacts is lower than in the original RESPECT-D study (Dietrich et al., 2004), in which 64 percent of depressed patients had follow-up contacts.
- After the initial care facilitator contact, service members had an average of 2.6 follow-up contacts, which falls slightly below RESPECT-Mil recommended guidelines.

- Nearly 80 percent of all monthly follow-up contacts were conducted early or on time.
- Ninety percent of monthly follow-up contacts had a clinical assessment recorded.

Similar to other collaborative care studies, care facilitators experienced challenges with establishing contact with a substantial proportion of service members after their initial primary care referral to RESPECT-Mil. Furthermore, care facilitators were unable to engage service members in the recommended number of follow-up contacts. Of the follow-up contacts that were made, a high proportion were conducted on time and included clinical assessments to track responses to treatment. Service members who had established contact with the care facilitator remained enrolled in RESPECT-Mil for approximately two months, on average, which is a shorter time frame than outlined by the program.

We then asked: *Are service members participating in the full course of recommended treatment? What is the degree of engagement in psychotropic medication, counseling, self-management goals, and psychoeducation?*

Regarding psychotropic medication:

- Approximately 39 percent of service members who established contact with the care facilitator reported starting psychotropic medication. Psychotropic medication use was relatively lower than rates found in comparable studies with ranges between 73 and 83 percent (Fortney, Pyne, Edlund, et al., 2007; Hedrick et al., 2003; Schnurr, Friedman, Oxman, et al., 2013).
- At baseline, only 9 percent of service members reported that they were taking or that their primary care provider had suggested that they take medication.[6] This increased to 53 percent by last follow-up contact.
- Among service members who had been prescribed medication, adherence rates stayed about the same from baseline (60 percent) to last follow-up contact (61 percent).

Regarding counseling:

- Twenty-three percent of service members who had contact with a care facilitator had started counseling while enrolled in RESPECT-Mil.
- At baseline, only 14 percent of service members were recorded as either attending counseling or having been referred to counseling by a primary care provider.[7] This increased to 67 percent by last follow-up contact.
- Among service members attending counseling appointments, approximately 30 percent reported "attending all," "almost always," or "often." This increased to 49 percent by the last follow-up contact. Comparable rates of engagement in counseling were found in the RESPECT-D study (Dietrich et al., 2004).

---

[6] This finding is based on responses to the question, "Are you taking or has any primary care provider suggested you take any prescribed medication for depression or PTSD?" Whether service members are taking medication or whether their primary care provider suggested that they take medication are distinct constructs. However, this study's analyses could not examine these constructs separately given how the medication engagement question is asked in FIRST-STEPS.

[7] The counseling engagement question similarly confounds the two constructs of whether service members are engaged in counseling and whether any primary care provider has recommended counseling.

Regarding self-management goals and psychoeducation:

- Sixty-seven percent of service members who made contact with a care facilitator reported working on self-management goals. This rate of engagement is substantially higher than found in a VA collaborative care study (Fortney, Enderle, et al., 2012).
- Sixty percent were recorded as having read psychoeducational materials. This figure is comparable to the 71 percent of individuals who reported being offered psychoeducational materials (a less stringent criteria) in RESPECT-D.

Overall, 46 percent of service members had started either psychotropic medication or counseling while enrolled in RESPECT-Mil. Although primary care provider recommendations for psychotropic medication and service member initiation of psychotropic medications appeared to increase over the course of RESPECT-Mil, only 39 percent of service members had started psychotropic medications, which is relatively lower than rates found in other collaborative care studies. Similarly, rates of attending counseling or having a primary care provider recommend counseling increased during the course of being enrolled in RESPECT-Mil. In total, 23 percent of service members were recorded as having started counseling while enrolled in RESPECT-Mil, which is comparable to some other collaborative care studies (Dietrich et al., 2004; Hedrick et al., 2003). More than 60 percent of service members were recorded as having engaged in self-management goals and in psychoeducation, rates that are comparable to or higher than those found in other collaborative care studies.

Efficacy

The RAND team used the same FIRST-STEPS data to examine outcomes associated with RESPECT-Mil. We summarize our findings in response to the following questions: *What proportion of service members experience improvement in depression and/or PTSD symptoms? What proportion shows improvement in functioning?*

- Forty-two percent of service members in the "depression prominent" category experienced a 50 percent reduction in depression symptoms from baseline to the last follow-up assessment. Other studies have reported a range of 19 percent to 53 percent of patients showing similar improvement.
- Thirty-three percent of service members in the "PTSD prominent" category experienced similar decreases in symptoms. In a civilian collaborative care study with PTSD patients, 50 percent experienced decreases in symptoms with a less stringent criterion (i.e., 40 percent reduction in symptoms) and with a longer follow-up period (six months) (Craske et al., 2011).
- Twenty-nine percent of service members in the "depression prominent" category experienced remission, which is within the range of other depression collaborative care studies, with rates of 26 percent to 30 percent (Dietrich et al., 2004; Fortney, Enderle, et al., 2012).
- Twenty-six percent of service members in the "PTSD prominent" category experienced remission. This rate is substantially higher than that found in the Re-Engineering Systems for the Primary Care Treatment of PTSD (RESPECT-PTSD) study (Schnurr, Friedman, Oxman, et al., 2013), which may have enrolled patients with greater levels of clinical symptom severity.

- Across the clinical status categories, the proportion of service members who reported no longer experiencing depression and/or PTSD-related impairment in functioning at their last follow-up visit ranged from 17 to 28 percent.

Overall, rates of treatment response and remission seen in RESPECT-Mil were within the range of other collaborative care studies. A slightly larger proportion of service members in the depression prominent category reported no longer experiencing functional impairment at the last follow-up assessment compared with service members in the PTSD prominent or depression plus PTSD prominent categories.

Aim 2: Facilitators and Barriers to Implementation

Based on interviews with providers (care facilitators, behavioral health champions, primary care champions, and primary care providers), we identified factors that facilitate or hinder the various provider roles.

Facilitators

- Screening for mental health needs is valued as a means of reaching a broader population that otherwise might not receive mental health care.
- Regular communication and consultation with the behavioral health champion eases primary care providers' comfort with prescribing and managing medication for depression and PTSD.
- Solid linkages between primary care providers and care facilitators facilitate successful care coordination.

Barriers

- Stigma (that is, fear of negative repercussions by one's unit and for career advancement) impedes engagement in mental health treatment.
- Some primary care providers do not buy into the program and refuse to refer service members to RESPECT-Mil.
- Short appointment times and heavy caseloads create challenging time constraints, especially for primary care providers and behavioral health champions.
- Primary care providers can experience discomfort with handling behavioral health issues. Many viewed certain behavioral health problems as requiring treatment outside of primary care.
- Insufficient coordination and communication between providers can pose problems. In particular, the handoff between the primary care provider and the care facilitator presented difficulties.
- Care facilitators are perpetually challenged in their ability to maintain contact with service members due to deployment, permanent change of station, block leave, and so on.
- Lack of engagement by top command is seen as a lost opportunity to strengthen the program, if not an outright barrier.

Interviews with the RESPECT-Mil Implementation Team also provided insight into factors that facilitate and impede their role in providing training, monitoring, and oversight of program implementation.

Facilitators

- Command support (e.g., Medical Command, Installation Command, chief of primary care, chief of family medicine) assists in the development of an implementation plan that is good for the site.
- Site performance reports are a valuable tool for monitoring and enforcing program fidelity.
- Monthly phone "coaching" calls provide sites with support around hiring, staff turnover, and training, as well as with problem solving around any implementation issues.

Barriers

- RESPECT-Mil Implementation Team staff are "too small" and "stretched too thin" to perform effectively.
- Unfilled provider positions due to long hiring processes and staff turnover can hinder program implementation.
- There are challenges in providing real-time feedback to sites due to delays in obtaining data from clinics as well as in creating and disseminating performance reports.

Aim 3: Sustainability of RESPECT-Mil

We also asked key Army and DoD stakeholders, many of whom are responsible for implementing health care initiatives in the Army, about sustainability issues regarding RESPECT-Mil, particularly in the context of the transition to the PCMH model of care that is now under way. The discussions focused on the following issues:

Addressing stigma in the Army. RESPECT-Mil was cited as a promising way to destigmatize mental health care, suggesting that the program meets an important need. Other comments noted the possibility of adapting RESPECT-Mil for other deployment environments and for explicitly targeting suicide prevention.

Meeting the mental health care needs of service members. There was general support among respondents, who saw value in the RESPECT-Mil program. At the same time, there was consensus that the time was ripe for a reevaluation of mental health initiatives. Circumstances have changed since RESPECT-Mil was first launched. In addition, future funding for mental health initiatives may not be as robust as once envisioned, suggesting a possible need to consolidate mental health programs and potentially integrate RESPECT-Mil with other initiatives. Further, though some considered RESPECT-Mil's performance monitoring system as advanced for Army medicine programs, others were more critical and stressed the need to examine the evidence base for the program and service member outcomes.

Transitioning to the PCMH model. Most respondents agreed that the RESPECT-Mil program would likely be integrated into the PCMH model over time, meaning that the program would lose its status as a separate program with fenced funding. However, some aspects of the program were perceived as valuable and worthy to be continued. In particular, respondents pointed to the screening aspect of RESPECT-Mil, as well as the continuing integration of primary care providers into behavioral health care, especially for medication management for depression and PTSD. In addition, the program's activities for monitoring and tracking patient progress were noted as strengths.

Interviews with the RESPECT-Mil Implementation Team identified other factors that may affect the sustainability of RESPECT-Mil. Factors include the amount and source of funding (e.g., U.S. Army Medical Command versus Defense Centers of Excellence), which can affect critical implementation processes like hiring, training, and the use of the FIRST-STEPS system; leadership support and buy-in; and the increased workload resulting from the expansion of services to dependents of service members, and to the Navy, Marines, and Air Force, which is occurring under the rollout of the PCMH.

Conclusions and Recommendations

Overall, our results indicate that RESPECT-Mil is performing in ways that are comparable to other primary care collaborative care efforts that have been analyzed in the published scientific literature. Of course, RESPECT-Mil is difficult to compare with other collaborative care studies because of differences in selection criteria for enrollment, settings, and types of interventions. Given this caveat, however, both processes of care and outcomes for RESPECT-Mil are generally comparable with those of other programs. Nonetheless, some aspects of program implementation lagged behind expectations delineated in the program design and manuals, indicating opportunities for improvement in the future.

Based on these results, we developed several recommendations for refining the RESPECT-Mil program and for improving the access and quality of behavioral health services for military service members. The highlights of these recommendations appear below.

Improving the Recognition and Assessment of Depression and PTSD

Consider ways to streamline screening and assessment. Routine screening is seen as a major strength of RESPECT-Mil. Potential areas where streamlining might be explored include bypassing clinical assessments among service members who have been recently screened and diagnosed by the program and finding ways to ease the administrative burden involved in conducting and recording assessments.

Determine the value of screening service members already enrolled in behavioral health care. Half of the positive screens were already in behavioral health care. Flagging service members who are experiencing clinically significant depression and/or PTSD symptoms despite receiving care in behavioral health settings may provide an opportunity to intervene to ensure that adequate levels of treatment are being obtained.

Enhance command support. Findings from stakeholder and RESPECT-Mil provider discussions indicated that service members may not report PTSD and depression symptoms during routine screening because of anticipated negative repercussions from their fellow service members and commanders. Due to the use of different screening and diagnostic instruments as well as scoring algorithms in other research studies, there are no benchmarks to accurately gauge whether service members are underreporting on RESPECT-Mil screening and diagnostic assessments. However, concerns regarding underreporting of PTSD and depression symptoms due to stigma have been well documented (Institute of Medicine, 2012). Continuing and enhancing command support for the RESPECT-Mil program, as well as other evidence-based programs for psychological health, may foster greater openness and disclosure of PTSD and depression among service members.

Explore expanding routine screening and evidence-based primary care management practices for depression and PTSD. Findings suggest that RESPECT-Mil is catching people who may have previously fallen through the cracks. Based on this observation, stakeholders and

RESPECT-Mil providers recommended that routine screening for PTSD and depression should be expanded to all primary care settings.

Improving Referrals and the Management of Depression and PTSD in Primary Care

Increase primary care provider engagement and comfort. RESPECT-Mil provider discussions revealed that some primary care providers do not feel comfortable managing the mental health needs of service members. Identified concerns include fears of being held liable for adverse behavioral health outcomes and beliefs that PTSD should be handled in behavioral health. Ways to increase primary care provider engagement in the program and comfort with addressing behavioral health needs could include monitoring individual primary care provider performance, providing additional training with primary care champions, and strengthening the consultative relationship with behavioral health champions, as well as structural or cultural changes to the primary care environment that better allow for the time and effort needed to address mental health issues.

Incentivize and support primary care champions. Primary care champions face severe constraints and need to demonstrate productivity outside the RESPECT-Mil program. Opportunities should be expanded for incentivizing and supporting those in the champion positions so that they can continue to train, monitor, and assist primary care providers in maintaining fidelity to the program.

Consider whether modifications are needed given the range of symptom severity among service members referred to the program. Of the service members referred to and enrolled in RESPECT-Mil, fewer than half met criteria for a probable depression or PTSD diagnosis. Further investigation is needed to understand the reasons for referral and enrollment of service members with no or minimal depression or PTSD symptoms.

Strengthen the handoff between the primary care provider and the care facilitator. A significant proportion of service members with mild to severe depression or PTSD symptoms (38 percent) who were referred to the program never established contact with the nurse serving as the care facilitator. More than half of these service members either withdrew from the program or could not be engaged or contacted. It would be helpful to explore strategies to prevent service member dropout after the initial primary care referral, including training primary care providers to better orient and introduce service members to the program as well as providing warm handoffs within clinics.

Facilitate engagement and communication with service members. Service members with mild to severe depression and/or PTSD who successfully established their initial contact with nurse care facilitators have an average of 2.6 subsequent follow-ups with the facilitators. Moreover, during the period of enrollment in the program, only 46 percent of service members report starting any medication or counseling. Given that the level of treatment engagement is below optimal for a substantial proportion of service members, strategies for facilitating engagement and communication should be explored. This may include the use of newer technologies for communication (e.g., texting, social media) as well training nurse care facilitators in motivational interviewing strategies.

Enlist command in support of service members' treatment engagement and adherence while recognizing that some service members may want to keep their treatment confidential. According to provider and stakeholder discussions, barriers to treatment engagement include service member concerns about the potential negative repercussions on job performance and career advancement, as well as the lack of flexibility and support on the part of commanders to accommodate treatment requirements (e.g., modifying schedules to attend treatment appointments). Enlisting the support of commanders could play an integral role in creating incentives for service members to engage in and adhere to treatment. Avenues that can be explored include educating commanders on the effect of policies that discourage treatment seeking among service members, building collaborative relationships between commanders and primary care providers, and promoting commander awareness of the program via trainings delivered by behavioral health champions or primary care champions.

Fortify communication between providers. Based on discussions with providers, several areas of communication between them were identified as possible targets for improvement. To strengthen the coordination of care among providers, the following could be considered: Explore ways to integrate and streamline record management systems (e.g., Armed Forces Health Longitudinal Technology Application, FIRST-STEPS), expand venues for communication outside the medical record systems (e.g., colocation, cross-unit meetings focused on service member care), and identify strategies to ensure that primary care providers are obtaining feedback (positive and negative) about the service members they have referred to RESPECT-Mil.

Ensure that the behavioral health champion role is adequately supported. Barriers to carrying out the responsibilities of behavioral health champions include severe constraints on staff time, competing priorities related to their primary occupational responsibilities within behavioral health, and few incentives to participate in RESPECT-Mil. In order to enable behavioral health champions to perform optimally, consider ways to provide adequate and protected time for RESPECT-Mil duties, incentivize participation in the program, and ensure efficient staffing of cases.

Consider enhancing the behavioral champion role. Behavioral health champions were depicted as functioning positively in their role as informal consultants to primary care providers regarding the diagnosis and management of depression and PTSD. Consideration may be given to enhancing the behavioral health champion role in providing more-intensive support to primary care providers. Expansion of the behavioral health champion role may occur through changes in location, availability, and incentives. Behavioral health champion engagement may be especially important during the initial phases of implementation, when primary care providers are being trained in the program and their comfort and skill level in managing behavioral health issues are developing.

Improving Quality Assurance Monitoring

Augment individualized and real-time performance feedback. Currently, no apparent, routinized protocol is in place to provide primary care providers or behavioral champions with performance feedback on fidelity to the program. Care facilitator performance can be monitored via FIRST-STEPS, but the type and frequency of feedback provided are unclear. For example, performance feedback for care facilitators could include the rate at which service members are being successfully connected to medication and counseling, engaging in the full course of recommended treatment, and appropriately referred to other behavioral resources. The development of targets for optimal performance for each provider role will be important so that sites can gauge their own performance against target metrics.

Create incentives for sites and providers to buy into quality improvement processes. More routine, localized, on-site monitoring may increase ownership and investment in quality improvement processes. In addition, localized monitoring may facilitate more real-time and personalized feedback, which is more challenging to conduct when the monitoring of all Army sites is centralized.

Continue support for the RESPECT-Mil Implementation Team or similar centralized quality improvement programs. The RESPECT-Mil Implementation Team data collection efforts on clinic screening and referral practices and care management activities via FIRST-STEPS allow for valuable tracking on implementation fidelity as well as program effectiveness. This is in line with one of the major recommendations issued in an Institute of Medicine report, *Treatment for Posttraumatic Stress Disorder in Military and Veteran Populations: Initial Assessment*, which called for the DoD and the VA to "institute programs of research to evaluate the efficacy, effectiveness, and implementation of all their PTSD screening, treatment, and rehabilitation services" (Institute of Medicine, 2012, p. 13).

Establish a self-monitoring process for the RESPECT-Mil Implementation Team oversight efforts. Ongoing evaluations of the relative merit and impact of different monitoring strategies (e.g., site visits, site calls) may be beneficial for targeting which activities should be continued and supported, particularly in light of limited resources.

Implementation of RESPECT-Mil Within the Military Health System

Given that RESPECT-Mil is slated to be the model that is used to implement behavioral health treatment within the PCMH, careful consideration is needed to determine the aspects of RESPECT-Mil that add value and can be preserved within the PCMH. Continued monitoring and oversight of the RESPECT-Mil program and the PCMH will be necessary as these programs change and adapt over time, since they have similar goals but different structural elements.

Conclusions

The real-world implementation of RESPECT-Mil in Army primary care settings is comparable to other collaborative care efforts that are often conducted under more tightly controlled research conditions. As with other collaborative care efforts, RESPECT-Mil encountered significant implementation barriers. Challenges included establishing initial contact with service members on referral to the program, procuring service member engagement in the full course of recommended treatment, obtaining provider buy-in, provider time constraints and competing demands, and the provision of oversight and accountability to program fidelity. Factors that facilitated the implementation of RESPECT-Mil included valuing routine screening for depression and PTSD as an effective way to reach service members who may otherwise fall through the cracks; behavioral health champions' support and consultations with primary care providers; and solid linkages between primary care providers and care facilitators. Our findings highlight key junctures where opportunities for engaging service members in needed treatment for depression or PTSD may be improved. Potential avenues for improving program fidelity include increasing the comfort of primary care providers and incentives to address depression and PTSD within primary care settings, ensuring warm handoffs between the initial primary care referral and the care facilitator in order to protect against dropouts, equipping providers with additional skills and strategies to improve treatment engagement, and providing individualized provider performance feedback. Even if perfect program fidelity were achieved, barriers such as stigma and lack of leadership support for recommended treatment plans are unlikely to be completely overcome without corresponding increases in organizational and policy support. Recommendations issued in this report are targeted at the provider, clinic administration, and military organizational levels on how to improve the implementation of primary care collaborative care programs aimed at enhancing mental health care. Recommendations are relevant to efforts currently under way to usher in the PCMH by building on the foundations and infrastructure developed by RESPECT-Mil.

Acknowledgments

We gratefully acknowledge the support of RESPECT-Mil Implementation Team members Charles Engel, Justin Curry, Sheila Barry, and Timothy McCarthy, who provided valuable guidance in the acquisition and deciphering of available program evaluation data. We especially thank the team for serving as collaborative partners who embraced RAND's commitment to objective and independent analysis. We would also like to express gratitude for our project monitor at the Defense Centers of Excellence for Psychological Health and Traumatic Brain Injury, Yonatan Tyberg. We appreciate the comments provided by our reviewers, Lisa Meredith and Paula P. Schnurr. Their constructive critiques were addressed, as part of RAND's rigorous quality assurance process, to improve the caliber of this report. We acknowledge the support and assistance of Deborah Scharf, David Adamson, and Carrie Farmer, as well as Sarah Hauer and Anna Smith, in the preparation of this report. We are also grateful for the time and informative input from the RESPECT-Mil providers, RESPECT-Mil Implementation Team staff, and various military health stakeholders who participated in our interviews.

CHAPTER ONE

Introduction

This report describes RAND's evaluation of the implementation of the Re-Engineering Systems of Primary Care Treatment in the Military (RESPECT-Mil). In this chapter, we provide an overview of the RESPECT-Mil program, its implementation within military installations, and the key aims of the present evaluation.

Background

During the decade following the September 11, 2001, terrorist attacks, approximately 2.6 million U.S. service members were deployed to support combat operations in Afghanistan (Operation Enduring Freedom [OEF]) and Iraq (Operation Iraqi Freedom [OIF] and Operation New Dawn [OND]) (U.S. Government Accountability Office [GAO], 2011). The U.S. military has been functioning at an unprecedented high operational tempo, as evidenced by the multiple deployments of more than a third of these U.S. service members and the extended period of conflict (GAO, 2011). The psychological toll of these protracted combat operations on U.S. service members has garnered increasing concern. Estimates indicate that up to a fifth of U.S. service members deployed to OEF and OIF may be affected by posttraumatic stress disorder (PTSD) and major depression.

The Department of Defense (DoD) has engaged in a series of efforts to ensure that the military health system is adequately positioned to address the psychological health needs of service members (see, e.g., Independent Review Group on Rehabilitative Care and Administrative Processes at Walter Reed Army Medical Center and National Naval Medical Center, 2007; President's Commission on Care for America's Returning Wounded Warriors, 2007; Task Force on Returning Global War on Terror Heroes, 2007). In 2006, the DoD Task Force on Mental Health was commissioned to conduct an investigation on how to improve the efficacy of psychological health services for members of the armed forces (Department of Defense Task Force on Mental Health, 2007).

One of the major findings highlighted by the task force is the continued and widespread stigma associated with mental health treatment in the military (Department of Defense Task Force on Mental Health, 2007). Concerns about negative repercussions with respect to career advancement and perceptions by one's unit have been identified as significant barriers to accessing care (Hoge, Auchterlonie, and Milliken, 2006; Schell and Marshall, 2008). Indeed, despite high rates of need, a substantial proportion of service members forgo mental health services. Among active duty service members who have probable PTSD or depression, nearly half have not sought any mental health care in the prior year (Schell and Marshall, 2008).

Consequently, one of the main recommendations issued by the task force is increasing the accessibility of mental health services by embedding mental health professionals in primary care settings, which may be less stigmatizing than specialty clinics for mental health (Department of Defense Task Force on Mental Health, 2007). Service members make an average of three primary care visits per year, with women and those with PTSD accessing primary care at even higher rates (Frayne et al., 2011). Identifying service members with unmet mental health needs in primary care and connecting them to services may be an effective means for increasing access to treatment.

Effective approaches to integrating mental health treatment within primary care settings have been established for the treatment of depression and anxiety in civilian settings (Archer et al., 2012; Thota et al., 2012). Though efforts to integrate mental health care into primary care settings have been well under way in the Department of Veterans Affairs (VA), most efforts target the treatment of depression (Felker et al., 2006; Fortney, Enderle, et al., 2012). Similar efforts to integrate mental health care within primary care settings in military treatment facilities (MTFs) with active duty service members have also been initiated, but they have not been evaluated extensively (Weinick et al., 2011).

In 2009, the Defense Centers of Excellence for Psychological Health and Traumatic Brain Injury (DCoE) requested RAND's assistance in assessing the effectiveness of DoD-sponsored programs aimed at promoting the psychological health of service members and their families. One of the programs selected for evaluation is RESPECT-Mil, a system of care designed to screen, assess, and treat PTSD and depression in Army primary care settings with active duty service members. This report details RAND's independent evaluation of the implementation of RESPECT-Mil. In the remaining sections of this chapter, we provide an overview of the core features of RESPECT-Mil, its implementation in the Army's MTFs, and the key aims of this implementation evaluation.

RESPECT-Mil Three Component Model (3CM)

RESPECT-Mil is based on a collaborative care approach to delivering mental health care within primary care settings (Engel et al., 2008). Though different variations exist, collaborative care models generally consist of health care system–level interventions that employ case managers to coordinate care between primary care providers (PCPs), patients, and mental health specialists (Thota et al., 2012). Case managers typically support PCPs by delivering patient psychoeducation, tracking patient treatment adherence and outcomes, and coordinating consultation with mental health specialists when treatment modifications are needed (e.g., medication side effects, treatment nonresponse). PCPs often implement routine screening and diagnosis for mental disorders, prescribe psychotropic medications, and, when necessary, refer service members to mental health specialists. Mental health specialists provide clinical consultation and decision support to PCPs. Collaborative care approaches have been found to be effective in improving the quality of care for depression in civilian and VA primary care settings (Chaney et al., 2011; Gilbody et al., 2006; Hedrick et al., 2003; Thota et al., 2012). Moreover, there is a growing evidence base for the effectiveness of collaborative care approaches for the treatment of anxiety, but relatively little research has specifically focused on PTSD or military populations (Archer et al., 2012).

RESPECT-Mil expands on a collaborative care model, the Re-Engineering Primary Care Treatment of Depression (RESPECT-D) (Dietrich et al., 2004). At the center of RESPECT-D is its Three Component Model (3CM), a systematic integrated team approach to depression care involving three core components: the prepared primary care clinician and practice, care management, and the collaborating mental health specialist. RESPECT-D was designed to account for the challenges involved in implementing and sustaining collaborative care programs in real-world settings that are devoid of intensive, externally funded research support. RESPECT-D is devised of practical, evidence-based clinical routines for depression management that are intended to facilitate broad dissemination using available resources within health care organizations. It was tested in five large health care organizations with 60 primary care practices and relied on established quality improvement programs to facilitate its implementation (Dietrich et al., 2004). Hallmarks of quality improvement programs include tracking performance quality via data collection, providing feedback to providers and administrators on performance quality indicators, and supporting providers and organizations in meeting performance targets through additional training, resources, and changes in organizational practices. RESPECT-D was found to substantially improve depression-related outcomes and treatment satisfaction compared with treatment as usual in primary care (Dietrich et al., 2004).

RESPECT-D has been adapted and tested for the treatment of PTSD in primary care clinics at VA medical centers (i.e., Re-Engineering Systems for the Primary Care Treatment of PTSD [RESPECT-PTSD]) (Schnurr, Friedman, Oxman, et al., 2013). In a randomized clinical trial, veterans who had been enrolled in RESPECT-PTSD versus treatment as usual exhibited no significant differences in PTSD treatment outcomes (Schnurr, Friedman, Oxman, et al., 2013). Although RESPECT-PTSD did not significantly affect PTSD symptoms, veterans enrolled in the program were more likely to engage in mental health visits and fill an antidepressant prescription. The VA population is characterized by more-severe and comorbid PTSD and they receive care in settings that differ from active duty service members (Institute of Medicine, 2012).

RESPECT-Mil builds on RESPECT-D by using the 3CM to improve the management of PTSD and depression care in the Army's primary care clinics.[1] Each component has been carefully outlined in RESPECT-Mil manuals created for each provider role (Barry and Oxman, 2008; Oxman, 2008). In the next section, we summarize the following three components according to the RESPECT-Mil model: (1) the PCP and prepared practice, (2) the RESPECT-Mil care facilitator (RCF), and (3) the behavioral health specialist, more commonly referred to as the *behavioral health champion* (BHC) (Engel et al., 2008). We also describe the role of the RESPECT-Mil Implementation Team (RMIT) and the efforts thus far related to the implementation of RESPECT-Mil. Figure 1.1 provides an overview of the interactions between providers and the RMIT, as well information that is collected to track implementation fidelity and treatment process and outcomes.

Primary Care Providers and the Prepared Practice

The PCP's role in the 3CM model of RESPECT-MIL is to recognize and assess service members who may be experiencing depression or PTSD, facilitate access to needed mental health treatment, and manage service members' care. Preparing the practice to implement the RESPECT-MIL program requires training and equipping the clinic staff with the tools and information needed to assist service members who may become engaged in the program. At each installation site, a PCP is selected to serve as the primary care champion (PCC), whose

---

[1]   At the time when this current implementation evaluation was commissioned, RESPECT-Mil had already been implemented in most Army installations, precluding a randomized clinical trial study.

Figure 1.1
Overview of RESPECT-Mil

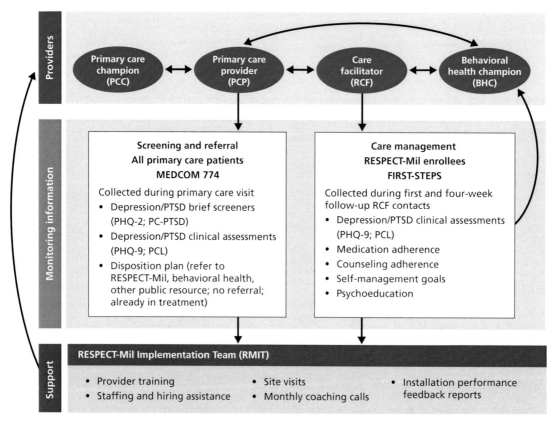

NOTE: PCL = Posttraumatic Stress Disorder Checklist—Civilian Version; FIRST-STEPS = Fast Informative Risk and Safety Tracker and Stepped Treatment Entry and Planning System.

RAND *RR588-1.1*

role is to oversee the PCPs at each clinic, supporting them in their role and acting as a liaison with the central RMIT (see the following for a description of the RMIT).

Screening for Depression and PTSD

One goal of RESPECT-MIL is to institute routine screening for depression and PTSD among service members attending primary care clinics or battalion aid stations. The integration of this process into clinical practice is achieved through operational meetings with the clinic administrators and staff during the preparation of the practice. Screening is incorporated into the clinical visit during the taking of vital signs. At that time, service members are given the U.S. Army Medical Command (MEDCOM) Form 774, which includes brief screeners for depression and PTSD (see Appendix A). Section I of the MEDCOM Form 774 contains a modified version of the Patient Health Questionnaire-2 (PHQ-2) (Kroenke, Spitzer, and Williams, 2003), a two-item brief screener for depression. The MEDCOM Form 774's modified version of the PHQ-2 employs "yes" or "no" responses instead of a 0 (not at all) to 3 (nearly every day) response scale. A positive screen for depression requires at least one "yes" response to either of the two PHQ-2 questions. Section II of the MEDCOM Form 774 is composed of the Primary Care PTSD

Screen (PC-PTSD, a four-item brief screener for PTSD) (Prins et al., 2003). A positive screen for PTSD requires at least two "yes" responses.

Establishing a Probable Diagnosis for Depression and PTSD

If a service member screens positive on the PHQ-2, a slightly longer measure, the Patient Health Questionnaire-9 (PHQ-9) (Kroenke, Spitzer, and Williams, 2001), is administered to aid in the probable diagnosis of depression and to determine the severity of symptoms. The PHQ-9 is based on criteria from the *Diagnostic and Statistical Manual of Mental Disorders, Fourth Edition, Text Revision, DSM-IV*; (American Psychiatric Association, 2000). The PHQ-9 contains nine items that assess the frequency with which depression symptoms were experienced over the past two weeks using a four-point scale, from 0 (not at all) to 3 (nearly every day) (see Appendix B). The PHQ-9 also employs a single functional impairment item that assesses the degree to which depression symptoms have made it difficult to function at work, at home, and with other people, using a four-point scale ranging from "not difficult at all" to "extremely difficult." Upon completion, the PCP or nursing staff member scores the self-administered questionnaire in order to establish the probable diagnosis and calculate a symptom severity score to help select and monitor treatment. See Appendix C for RESPECT-Mil scoring guidelines.

If a service member screens positive on the PC-PTSD, the Posttraumatic Stress Disorder Checklist—Civilian Version (PCL) (Weathers et al., 1993) is administered to assess the probable diagnosis and severity of PTSD. The PCL is also a self-administered questionnaire, which incorporates the *DSM-IV* criteria for PTSD. The PCL contains 17 items and evaluates symptoms in three PTSD symptom categories: intrusion, avoidance, and arousal. It assesses the degree to which symptoms have been experienced in the past month using a five-point scale ranging from 0 (not at all) to 4 (extremely).[2] In addition to the PCL, service members who screen positive on the PC-PTSD are administered the single functional impairment item from the PHQ-9 with respect to PTSD symptoms, as well as the PHQ-9 item on suicidal ideation (see Appendix D). RESPECT-Mil guidelines for establishing a probable PTSD diagnosis and calculating the PTSD symptom severity are provided in Appendix E.

Following the administration of the relevant clinical instruments, a clinical interview and a suicide-and-violence assessment are completed before the PCP makes a diagnosis. During the interview, the PCP asks service members about suicidal ideations, intent, or plans using a progressive set of suicide screening questions to assign a suicide risk level (low, intermediate, or high). The PCP then uses the risk assessment in addition to the score from the PHQ-9 to make a provisional diagnosis and recommend treatment. A list of effective antidepressants along with therapeutic dose ranges, suggested initial dose, and advantages versus disadvantages are provided to PCPs during the preparation phase of implementation of RESPECT-Mil. PCPs may rely on this list when making treatment recommendations to service members. In addition to treatment recommendations, PCPs encourage a self-management plan in which service members select an activity to work on each week to support positive coping (e.g., engaging in physical activity, spending time with supportive people). PCPs also offer the service of a nurse RCF to help monitor symptoms and side effects and to encourage treatment and plan adherence. If the services of the RCF are requested by service members, then a referral into RESPECT-Mil

---

[2] RESPECT-Mil changed the scoring range for the PCL and uses a 0 to 4 response set instead. We report PCL findings using the 0 to 4 scoring range.

is completed by the PCP. A similar protocol is in place for the treatment of PTSD. The PCL is used in place of the PHQ-9 to aid in the diagnosis of and treatment options for PTSD.

Acute, Continuation, and Maintenance Phases of Treatment

After being referred into RESPECT-Mil, the acute phase of treatment begins, which involves PCPs working with RCFs and BHCs to evaluate treatment response, modify treatment among those with suboptimal responses, and strive for the remission of symptoms. For depression, remission is defined as a reduction of the PHQ-9 score to less than 5, along with no functional impairment. For PTSD, remission is defined as a reduction of the PCL score to less than 11, along with no functional impairment. After remission is attained, service members enter into the continuation and maintenance phases of treatment. During the continuation phase, the goal is to keep service members in a state of remission. For service members on medication, RESPECT-Mil recommends that they continue to take the same medication and dose for four to nine months after achieving remission. During the maintenance phase, service members are provided education on how to recognize the early signs of relapse and to request an appointment with their PCPs or behavioral health providers. Referral for formal psychiatric consultation is recommended for service members who have the following: a suicide plan, comorbid substance abuse, hallucinations or delusional thinking, failure to respond to two trials of medication of adequate dose and duration, or serious or prolonged difficulty in performing military duties.

RESPECT-Mil Care Facilitator

The role of the RCF is to support the service member through the course of treatment and to support the PCP by promoting service member adherence to the treatment plan. The RCF provides service members with psychoeducation, supports their treatment preferences, and monitors adherence and response to treatment. As a liaison between the service member and the PCP, the RCF communicates the service member's experience to the PCP and ensures that the service member's needs are addressed. The care facilitation process begins after the PCP has made a diagnosis of depression or PTSD and the service member has opted for care facilitation services. According to the 3CM protocol, the RCF then makes contact with the service member within seven to ten days of the referral to RESPECT-Mil. PCPs typically complete referrals through the military's electronic health record, Armed Forces Health Longitudinal Technology Application (AHLTA). In the initial referral note sent to RCFs via AHLTA, PCPs will include information about the reason for the referral, clinical assessment scores, and details of the initial treatment plan (e.g., medication type and dose, counseling, self-management goal). When offices are colocated, service members are introduced to the RCF directly by the PCP. In the 3CM, the facilitation model is designed to be telephonic; however, in-person clinic visits are sometimes employed to increase access for service members.

During the initial encounter, the RCF explains his or her role as part of the service member's care team, reviews the details of the treatment plan, encourages treatment adherence, and schedules follow-ups in person or on the phone at four-week intervals. The RCF monitors treatment progress at four-week intervals, using the PHQ-9 for depression, the PCL for PTSD, and a suicidal risk assessment, until the service member reaches remission. Also, should the need arise, RCFs are available to service members between scheduled follow-up contacts. After each follow-up contact, the RCF completes notes on service member's treatment progress, adherence, and concerns, which are sent to the PCP via AHLTA using the Telephone Consults

(T-Cons) module. RCF notes are also recorded in the Fast Informative Risk and Safety Tracker and Stepped Treatment Entry and Planning System (FIRST-STEPS), an electronic case-management tracking system that records all service member contacts, PHQ-9 and PCL scores and changes, progress with self-management goals, psychotropic medication and counseling use, changes in medication and counseling adherence, and suicidal risk assessments. RCFs are registered nurses, and one RCF is allotted for every 6,000 eligible service members.

FIRST-STEPS

FIRST-STEPS is an electronic case-management tracking tool designed for use by RCFs and BHCs. FIRST-STEPS contains records on RCF contacts, clinical assessments, psychotropic medication and counseling adherence, engagement in psychoeducation and self-management goals, and the final dispositions of case closures. FIRST-STEPS is designed to facilitate the weekly staffing sessions in which RCFs and BHCs review select cases of service members who are enrolled in RESPECT-Mil. FIRST-STEPS automatically flags cases that need to be staffed based on treatment adherence barriers (e.g., medication side effects, waiting lists for counseling), lack of symptom improvement, suicidal ideation, or when remission has occurred. The flagged cases are reviewed with the BHC, who makes recommendations for the care of the service member. Those recommendations are then communicated to the PCP by the RCF via an AHLTA T-Cons. Depending on the staffing recommendations, the BHC may decide to contact the PCP. The PCP then uses his or her own discretion in adhering to the recommendations of the BHC regarding the service member's treatment plan.

Behavioral Health Champion

As prescribed by the 3CM, the BHC is a psychiatrist who serves as a component of the service member's care team. The BHC provides clinical and pharmacotherapy advice to the PCP, discusses the service member's progress with the RCF, and facilitates referrals to specialty care when indicated or requested. BHCs and RCFs discuss their assigned service members in weekly telephonic or in-person meetings. The service member's scores on clinical assessments (e.g., PHQ-9, PCL), symptoms, treatment adherence, and barriers to receiving care are discussed. The BHC reviews the information with the RCF and makes clinical recommendations for management based on the information presented and clinical judgment. All service members are staffed with the BHC before their cases are closed out of RESPECT-Mil. Recommendations are communicated to the PCP by the RCF via the service member health record in AHLTA. PCPs are able to make treatment changes based on the recommendations at their own discretion. If there are follow-up questions from the PCP, they are relayed to the BHC via the RCF. BHCs and PCPs can also communicate directly with each other via phone, email, or in person. For service members with depression, if remission is not achieved after two adequate trials of antidepressants and/or 20 to 30 weeks of psychological counseling, the BHC may recommend a formal or informal psychiatric consultation for diagnostic and management purposes. BHCs may also make similar referrals for service members being treated for PTSD who have not achieved remission following two adequate trials of pharmacotherapy and/or 24 weeks of psychological counseling.

RESPECT-Mil Implementation Team and Oversight

In 2007, MEDCOM issued Operation Order 07-34, which mandated the formation of the RMIT to provide program management, oversight, leadership, training, mentorship, and assistance to Army installations assigned to implement RESPECT-Mil (U.S. Army Medical Command, 2007). The RMIT is responsible for leading the worldwide implementation effort and has two missions:

- Oversee and implement training of the program to all relevant personnel.
- Facilitate and manage program implementation at all designated sites.

Within this capacity, the RMIT functions much like quality improvement programs established in civilian health care organizations. The RMIT performs a variety of responsibilities to support implementation and monitoring of fidelity to the program, including preparing the practice settings, assisting with hiring and staffing, training providers and champions, conducting coaching calls and site assessment visits, and providing performance feedback to installations.

The RMIT functions within the Deployment Health Clinical Center under DoD. It consists of individuals from various backgrounds (e.g., psychologists, psychiatrists, nurses), who are each responsible for different tasks related to the implementation and oversight of RESPECT-Mil. For example, there is a behavioral health proponent, who is responsible for training BHCs. The primary care proponent trains PCCs. Another RMIT member trains RCFs and facilitates monthly coaching calls with sites. Various RMIT members conduct site visits on an as-needed basis to assist sites lacking additional support in implementing RESPECT-Mil. There are also program evaluation and information technology RMIT members; they analyze FIRST-STEPS and clinic data, produce site reports, and troubleshoot problems with the system.

Implementation of RESPECT-Mil in Army Treatment Facilities

After an initial pilot was conducted to test the feasibility of RESPECT-Mil at the Womack Army Medical Center in Fort Bragg, North Carolina (Engel et al., 2008), the Army surgeon general in 2007 directed the dissemination of RESPECT-Mil to 15 Army MTF sites, involving 43 primary care clinics. The 15 Army sites were funded to hire one or two RCFs and an administrative assistant to facilitate the implementation of the program (Engel et al., 2008).

The implementation of RESPECT-Mil was rolled out in the following phases:

- Phase 1: preparing the sites
- Phase 2: training for personnel and initial implementation
- Phase 3: training for Army PCPs
- Phase 4: implementation and expansion

Phase 1: Preparing the Sites

In preparing for program implementation, MTF sites were expected to coordinate with the Office of the Surgeon General (OTSG), the Regional Medical Command (RMC), and satellite clinics to collect data on the need for care and the capacity to provide care at the installation where the MTF was located (U.S. Army Medical Command, 2007). Types of data to be collected included estimates of the number of primary care clinics, active duty enrollees and PCPs at each clinic, associated battalion aid stations, sick call and regular clinic visits per month, installation behavioral health and related psychosocial support resources, preexisting behavioral health resources integrated into primary care clinics, and the nature of specialty care programs specifically addressing depression and PTSD.

Table 1.1
Timeline for the Preparation Phase of Dissemination Sites

January–June 2007	May–September 2007	August–December 2007
Fort Drum, New York	Fort Benning, Georgia	Fort Lewis, Washington
Fort Stewart, Georgia	Fort Bliss, Texas	Vicenza, Italy
Fort Campbell, Kentucky	Fort Polk, Louisiana	Vilseck, Germany
Fort Hood, Texas	Fort Riley, Kansas	Schweinfurt, Germany
Fort Bragg, North Carolina	Fort Carson, Colorado	Schofield Barracks, Hawaii

According to Operation Order 07-34, the site preparation phase for the initial dissemination installations was scheduled to occur during the first year of implementation, following the timeline in Table 1.1.

Phase 2: Training for Personnel and Initial Implementation

The RMIT held two-day training workshops during the same time frame as the site preparation phase. RCFs, administrative assistants, PCCs, and BHCs attended the training sessions. A train-the-trainer method was used so that trainees learned the material comprehensively and gained experience that they could apply when training other personnel at their home stations. Operation Order 07-34 directed MTF site leaders to draft instructions for processes related to the preparation of sites, including the development of staff and operational communications strategies and protocols, tactics for oversight, service member tracking, and data collection. MTF site leaders were tasked with the responsibility of systematically assessing their program's adherence to the RESPECT-Mil design by using fidelity checklists developed by the RMIT. It was recommended that new PCPs and other relevant personnel go through RESPECT-Mil training as part of their orientation in order to minimize disruption to the program when staff turnover occurred.

Phase 3: Training Army Primary Care Providers

The RMIT began a RESPECT-Mil training program for Army PCPs in 2007 and continued through 2008 (U.S. Army Medical Command, 2007). The surgeon general RESPECT-Mil project officer directed the Army Medical Department Center and School, the RMIT, and the family medicine and behavioral health consultants to the surgeon general to develop training materials and a training plan on depression, PTSD, and RESPECT-Mil for PCPs throughout the Army (U.S. Army Medical Command, 2007). The purpose of the training was to enhance PCPs' abilities to assess and treat depression and PTSD in the primary care environment.

Phase 4: Implementation and Expansion

During the implementation phase, RESPECT-Mil staff and the RMIT continued with training, site visits, program monitoring and evaluation, and performance reporting (U.S. Army Medical Command, 2007). In February 2010, Operation Order 10-25 was issued, directing the expansion of RESPECT-Mil to an additional 19 installations (U.S. Army Medical Command, 2010). The site preparation and expansion phase for the additional installations was scheduled to occur according to the timeline in Table 1.2.

By the summer of 2012, RESPECT-Mil had expanded to 37 U.S. Army installations and more than 90 clinics (Deployment Health Clinical Center, 2012). As of 2012, RESPECT-Mil

Table 1.2
Timeline for the Preparation Phase of Expansion Sites

January–August 2010	January–August 2010	September–April 2010
Bamberg, Germany	Fort Eustis, Virginia	Fort Sam Houston, Texas
Baumholder, Germany	Fort Gordon, Georgia	Fort Sill, Oklahoma
Katterbach, Germany	Fort Jackson, South Carolina	Fort Leavenworth, Kansas
Wiesbaden, Germany	Fort Knox, Kentucky	Fort Leonard Wood, Missouri
	Fort Rucker, Alabama	Fort Huachuca, Arizona
	U.S. Military Academy, West Point, New York	Fort Irwin, California
	Walter Reed Army Medical Center, Washington, D.C.	Fort Wainwright, Alaska
		Brian Allgood, Korea

was beginning to undergo a tri-service expansion to provide services to the Air Force and the Navy in addition to the Army.

New Developments

Patient-Centered Medical Home and RESPECT-Mil

In January 2011, Operation Order 11-20 put into effect the implementation of the Army Patient Centered Medical Home (PCMH) (Tricare Management Activity, 2011). The concept of a PCMH was initially introduced by the American Academy of Pediatrics in 1967. In 2007, a consensus statement on the joint principles of the PCMH was developed and endorsed by the American Academy of Pediatrics, the American Academy of Family Physicians, the American College of Physicians, and the American Osteopathic Association (Rittenhouse and Shortell, 2009). PCMH is a team-based model in which the PCP is responsible for ensuring comprehensive and coordinated care in collaboration with specialty health care and other professional services (National Committee for Quality Assurance, 2011). Under the PCMH, the integration of behavioral health services within the Army's primary care settings continues to use aspects of RESPECT-Mil but through the new configuration of the PCMH-Behavioral Health Team (Deployment Health Clinical Center, 2012). In the PCMH-Behavioral Health Team, RCFs are called behavioral health case managers (BHCMs) and provide care facilitation for the health care team and the PCPs. The PCMH-Behavioral Health Team also includes internal behavioral health consultants (IBHCs), typically psychologists or social workers, who serve as part of the primary care team. IBHCs provide real-time consultation to PCPs as well as brief, time-limited interventions, such as behavioral activation, smoking cessation, mood management strategies, sleep hygiene guidance, and relaxation training. In addition, in the PCMH-Behavioral Health Team, RESPECT-Mil BHCs are known as external behavioral health consultants. In contrast to RESPECT-Mil, which supported only active duty service members, PCMH also supports service members' family members who are adult beneficiaries. IBHCs are available to share in the responsibilities of the additional workload, while the BHCMs attend to individuals who are likely to benefit from extended contact. The role of the BHCMs continues to be to assist PCPs and the health care team by providing continuity of care by monitoring behavioral health symptoms, medication side effects, and treatment adherence issues through regular phone contact with patients. BHCMs also ensure timely treatment from team decisions by facilitating the communication of important patient information to providers during team meetings.

STEPS-UP

As part of a five-year research project (2009–2014), the RMIT and outside collaborators at RTI International, RAND Corporation, and six Army MTFs are developing and testing an enhancement to RESPECT-Mil called Stepped Enhancement of PTSD Services Using Primary Care, or STEPS-UP, which is funded by the Congressionally Directed Medical Research Program. In this project RESPECT-Mil is enhanced by RCF training in motivational interviewing and behavioral activation, telephone-based psychotherapy and centralized care facilitation for service members who have difficulty making appointments during regular business hours, and enhanced access to evidence-based psychotherapy through web-based interventions for depression and PTSD. The project was ongoing in 2015 in six MTFs (Fort Bliss, Fort Bragg, Fort Campbell, Fort Carson, Joint Base Lewis-McChord, and Fort Stewart), with service members randomized to receive STEPS-UP or RESPECT-Mil. Results are expected to show whether these enhancements in STEPS-UP can improve outcomes over and above those observed in RESPECT-Mil, and are expected in 2015.

Purpose and Key Aims of This Study

The purpose of this study is to conduct an evaluation of the implementation of RESPECT-Mil. With the program having been stood up in more than 90 Army primary care clinics across 37 installations, RESPECT-Mil represents one of the largest real-world endeavors to implement collaborative care on a mass scale. By focusing the current study on evaluating the implementation of RESPECT-Mil, we will be able to examine the degree to which the program is reaching service members, areas that could be further strengthened, and salient issues related to integrating mental health treatment in the Army's primary care settings. Lessons learned may inform other current efforts to integrate mental health care into military primary care settings, including the rollout of the PCMH.

   This implementation evaluation had the following key aims: (1) Assess the degree to which RESPECT-Mil is being implemented in the Army's primary care settings; (2) identify facilitators and barriers to the implementation of RESPECT-Mil; and (3) examine factors associated with the sustainability of collaborative care programs such as RESPECT-Mil from the perspective of key stakeholders within the military health system.

   We map these three aims onto the RE-AIM (Reach, Efficacy, Adoption, Implementation, Maintenance) framework (Glasgow, Vogt, and Boles, 1999). The RE-AIM framework has been used as a model for evaluating the implementation or translation of evidence-based practices into real-world settings (Meyer et al., 2012; Rogers et al., 2013). According to the RE-AIM framework, the implementation and public health impact of an evidence-based intervention depends on several factors: the scope and extent to which the intervention *reach*es the targeted population; the *efficacy* of the intervention in yielding positive outcomes; the degree of *adoption* of the intervention across a substantial proportion of settings; the level of *implementation* fidelity with respect to whether the intervention is being delivered as designed; and the viability of the long-term *maintenance* (or sustainability) of the intervention.

For aim 1, we examined the implementation of RESPECT-Mil in relation to the *reach*, *adoption*, *implementation* fidelity, and *efficacy* of the program. We outline the questions asked to assess each of these domains.

To determine the *reach* of RESPECT-Mil, we asked the following questions:

- To what extent does RESPECT-Mil facilitate the identification of service members with mental health needs?
- To what degree does RESPECT-Mil support referrals to needed mental health treatment?

To examine the level of *adoption* of RESPECT-Mil across Army installations, we asked:

- How do Army installations vary with respect to the identification and referral of service members with mental health needs?

To assess the level of *implementation* fidelity, we posed the following questions:

- To what extent is RESPECT-Mil enrolling service members with depression and/or PTSD?
- Is RESPECT-Mil being delivered as intended? For example, to what extent are RCFs able to implement their responsibilities as outlined by the program protocol?
- To what degree are service members engaging in psychoeducation, psychotropic medication, counseling, and self-management goals? Are service members participating in the full course of recommended treatment?

To investigate the *efficacy* or positive outcomes associated with RESPECT-Mil, we explored the following:[3]

- What proportion of service members experience improvement in depression and/or PTSD symptoms?
- What proportion of service members show improvement in functioning?

Aims 2 and 3 address the *maintenance* of collaborative care programs such as RESPECT-Mil by identifying factors that facilitate, hinder, and sustain implementation.

Organization of This Report

In Chapter Two, we describe in detail the methodological approaches employed to carry out the key aims of this evaluation. Chapters Three through Six contain the findings resulting from

---

[3] The efficacy of an intervention can be tested using a variety of study designs. A randomized controlled trial in which PTSD and depression outcomes are compared among service members who are randomly assigned to RESPECT-Mil or usual care is considered the most rigorous test of efficacy. However, this was not possible given that the program had already been implemented throughout most of the Army installations before the start of the evaluation. This evaluation naturalistically investigated changes in clinical symptoms and functioning to examine the impact of the program on participants.

the evaluation. Chapter Seven concludes with a summary of the main findings and recommendations that may enhance the implementation of collaborative care programs like RESPECT-Mil. The recommendations are based on the findings that resulted from the three study aims and are organized according to major components and processes common to collaborative care programs. Specifically, the recommendations addressed areas for potential improvement with respect to the 3CM (i.e., PCPs and the prepared practice, the care facilitator, and the BHC), performance monitoring, and institutional support for the program.

CHAPTER TWO

Methodological Approach

In this chapter, we describe the methodological and analytical approaches used to carry out the following three key aims of this study:

1. Assess the degree to which RESPECT-Mil is being implemented in the Army's primary care settings.
2. Identify facilitators and barriers to the implementation of RESPECT-Mil.
3. Examine the sustainability of RESPECT-Mil from the perspective of key stakeholders within the military health system.

To accomplish these aims, we employed five complementary methods: (1) an analysis of Monthly Screening and Referral Clinic Reports; (2) an analysis of data from FIRST-STEPS, an electronic case-management tool designed for RESPECT-Mil; (3) discussions with RESPECT-Mil providers; (4) discussions with RMIT members; and (5) discussions with key stakeholders within the military health system. Table 2.1 provides a crosswalk between each of the methods used to inform the different aims. The remainder of this chapter is organized around each aim, and within each aim we provide detailed descriptions of the methods and approaches used.

Aim 1: Assess the Degree of RESPECT-Mil Implementation

For aim 1, we developed indicators to assess the reach, adoption, implementation, and efficacy of RESPECT-Mil by relying on two data sources that the RMIT collects to track program

Table 2.1
Crosswalk Between Study Aims and Methods

Method	Aim 1: Assess the Degree of RESPECT-Mil Implementation	Aim 2: Identify Facilitators and Barriers to RESPECT-Mil Implementation	Aim 3: Examine the Sustainability of RESPECT-Mil
Monthly Screening and Referral Clinic Reports analysis	X		
FIRST-STEPS analysis	X		
RESPECT-Mil provider discussions		X	
RMIT discussions		X	X
Military health system stakeholder discussions			X

fidelity—namely, Monthly Screening and Referral Clinic Reports and FIRST-STEPS data. Data were extracted from these two sources for the period of August 2011 to March 2012. August 2011 is when the Monthly Screening and Referral Clinic Reports incorporated the collection of separate screening and referral information for PTSD and depression. Prior to this time, the reports contained only aggregated information across the two mental health conditions. March 2012 is when the data from the reports and FIRST-STEPS were transferred to RAND. We focused our evaluation on the data from the specified time frame because this allowed us to report on program implementation across the specific type of mental health condition being addressed (i.e., PTSD, depression, or both). Data from the reports and FIRST-STEPS were analyzed for 37 U.S. Army installations with 84 primary care clinics. We excluded six primary care clinics that were in the initial phases of implementing RESPECT-Mil. In the next section, we provide a more detailed description of the two data sources and the analytic approaches applied to these data.

Data Sources

Monthly Screening and Referral Clinic Reports

As described earlier, RESPECT-Mil primary care clinics use the MEDCOM Form 774 to screen service members for depression and PTSD. In addition to the depression and PTSD screener questions,[1] the MEDCOM Form 774 is also used to document relevant clinical information, including depression and PTSD clinical assessment scores, suicidal risk assessments, diagnostic information (e.g., probable depression and/or PTSD), treatment plans, and a final disposition plan (e.g., refer the service member to RESPECT-Mil, behavioral health, or another resource) (see Appendix A). At the end of each month, RESPECT-Mil primary care clinics are asked to provide to the RMIT summative information based on completed MEDCOM Forms 774. The RMIT uses these Monthly Screening and Referral Clinic Reports to track program fidelity across installations and clinics. The RMIT maintains a database of all the Monthly and Referral Clinic Reports and issues periodic performance reports to sites with individualized feedback on program fidelity. The Monthly Screening and Referral Clinic Report data used for the analyses contained information on a total of 647,642 service member visits.

FIRST-STEPS Case-Management Tool

FIRST-STEPS, the electronic case-management tracking tool designed for use by RCFs and BHCs, contains records on RCF service member contacts, clinical assessments, treatment plans, medication and counseling adherence, engagement in self-management goals, and case closure dispositions. RAND obtained FIRST-STEPS data with deidentified service members from the U.S. Army Medical Information Technology Center. The RMIT has not had access to the kind of individual-level data obtained for the current evaluation, which has precluded a more fine-grained assessment of the implementation of RESPECT-Mil as is provided here. For the purposes of this study, FIRST-STEPS data were analyzed for service member cases opened and closed between August 2011 and March 2012. For service member cases not yet closed during this period, we included only those that were opened before October 2011 to ensure a minimum six-month period of treatment. This resulted in a total sample size of 3,403 service members who were included in the analyses using the FIRST-STEPS data.

---

[1] The MEDCOM Form 774 employs the PHQ-2 and PC-PTSD as brief screeners for depression and PTSD, respectively.

Analytic Plan

The following section describes the analytic plan for deriving implementation indicators for the reach, adoption, implementation fidelity, and efficacy of RESPECT-Mil. To assist with the interpretation of the derived implementation indicators, we compare our findings with other collaborative care studies about depression and PTSD, which we review alongside the results of aim 1 in Chapter Three of the report.

Reach

To determine the reach of RESPECT-Mil, we relied on the Monthly Screening and Referral Clinic Report data. Table 2.2 provides a list of definitions for constructs and measures used to operationalize indicators for reach. Outlined below are the indicators that are used to address the question: *To what extent does RESPECT-Mil facilitate the recognition of service members with mental health needs?*

- number and percentage of service member primary care visits that were screened for depression and PTSD (*visits screened*)
- percentage of screened visits that resulted in a positive screen for depression and/or PTSD (*positive screen*)
- percentage of positive screens resulting in a probable depression and/or PTSD diagnosis (*positive screen resulting in a probable diagnosis*)
- percentage of screened visits resulting in a probable depression and/or PTSD diagnosis (*visits screened resulting in a probable diagnosis*).

Another aspect of RESPECT-Mil's reach can also be considered in terms of the following question: *To what degree does RESPECT-Mil support referrals to needed mental health treatment?* To answer this question, we reviewed the final disposition of all positive screens, which are coded according to the following categories: referrals accepted, referrals declined, no referral, and already in treatment. Definitions for these categories are provided in Table 2.2.

Adoption

To gauge the degree to which RESPECT-Mil is being adopted across installations, we looked at the same reach indicators described in Table 2.2 for each site to answer the question: *How do Army installations vary with respect to the identification and referral of service members with mental health needs?*

Adoption indicators could only be derived from Monthly Screening and Referral Clinic Report data, which contain installation site information. Adoption indicators could not be derived for other components of RESPECT-Mil because FIRST-STEPS data do not record installation site information.

Implementation

To assess how key components of RESPECT-Mil are being implemented, we used FIRST-STEPS data to examine several aspects of the program. We describe the aspects of program implementation investigated in this study.

To What Extent Is RESPECT-Mil Enrolling Service Members with Depression and/or PTSD?

One unique facet that sets RESPECT-Mil apart from other collaborative care efforts is that the program does not exclusively focus on either depression or PTSD. Rather, RESPECT-Mil is

Table 2.2
Constructs and Definitions for Reach Indicators

Construct/Measure	Definition
Visits screened	PHQ-2 and PC-PTSD administered and recorded during primary care visit.[a]
Positive screen	Screened visits resulted in one or both of the following conditions: • At least 1 of 2 items on the PHQ-2 are endorsed. • At least 2 of 4 items on the PC-PTSD are endorsed.
Positive screen resulting in a probable diagnosis	Positive screens resulted in a probable depression and/or PTSD diagnosis as recorded on the MEDCOM Form 774.
Visits screened resulting in a probable diagnosis	Screened visits resulted in a probable depression and/or PTSD diagnosis as recorded on the MEDCOM Form 774.
Referrals accepted	Referral was accepted to any of the following: • RESPECT-Mil • Behavioral specialist • Another psychosocial resource (e.g., Military OneSource).
Referrals declined	Referral was declined to any of the following: • RESPECT-Mil • Behavioral specialist • Another psychosocial resource (e.g., Military OneSource).
No referral	No referral was made due to one of the following: • Behavioral health need that will be addressed in primary care • No behavioral health treatment need identified.
Already in treatment	No referral was made because service member already being followed by: • RESPECT-Mil • Behavioral specialist • Another psychosocial resource (e.g., Military OneSource).

[a] PHQ-2 and PC-PTSD are the brief screeners administered for depression and PTSD, respectively.

designed to screen for both depression and PTSD and provides guidelines and support for the treatment of both conditions. Thus, one aspect of program implementation that we explore is the clinical presentation of service members who are being enrolled and treated in RESPECT-Mil. We classified service members according to the clinical symptoms that were most prominently presented during the initial clinical assessment. We derived the following categories to indicate service members' baseline clinical status: depression prominent, PTSD prominent, and depression plus PTSD prominent (from herein referred to as DEP+PTSD).

To be classified as depression prominent, service members had to present with one of the following conditions: probable diagnosis of depression only, minor depression or mild major depression only, or moderately severe or severe major depression only. RESPECT-Mil provides scoring instructions along with recommended treatment guidelines for the different depression clinical severity levels, which are derived from initial PHQ-9 scores (see Appendix C). To be classified as PTSD prominent, service members had to present with one of the following conditions: probable diagnosis of PTSD only, mild PTSD only, or moderate or severe PTSD only. Appendix E contains RESPECT-Mil's scoring instructions and recommended treatment guidelines for the various PTSD clinical severity levels, which are based on the initial PCL score. To be classified as DEP+PTSD, service members had to present with one of the following conditions: probable depression and PTSD diagnosis or mild to severe depression and PTSD. We examined whether enrollment, treatment process, or treatment outcomes varied according to the baseline clinical status categories. Table 2.3 provides a summary of our derived baseline clinical status categories.

To What Extent Are RCFs Able to Carry Out Their Responsibilities as Outlined by the Program Protocol?

As described previously, a major component of RESPECT-Mil involves the role of the RCF in supporting treatment adherence and monitoring treatment response. Table 2.4 lists the constructs and measures developed to examine the implementation of program components that occur through RCF contacts with service members. To assess the degree and nature of RCF contacts, we examined the following:

- the percentage of cases in which no RCF contact was established after a referral to RESPECT-Mil (*no RCF contact*)
- among service members who had established contact with RCFs, the percentage of cases in which RCFs' first contact with service members occurred within 14 days of the initial primary care RESPECT-Mil referral (*RCF first contact*)
- mean number of RCF follow-up contacts (*RCF follow-up contacts*)
- the percentage of early, on time, and late RCF follow-up contacts (*timely RCF follow-up contacts*)
- the percentage of RCF follow-up contacts in which clinical assessments were administered and recorded (*follow-up assessment recorded*)
- the mean number of days enrolled in RESPECT-Mil (*number of days in the program*).

Are Service Members Participating in the Full Course of Treatment?

A core feature of RESPECT-Mil is the facilitation of service members' engagement in psychotropic medication treatment, counseling, self-management goals, and psychoeducation. Via FIRST-STEPS, RCFs administer a number of questions during first and follow-up contacts to monitor service member engagement across these treatment domains. In the next three sections we outline the implementation indicators derived from FIRST-STEPS data to examine questions about the degree of uptake of RESPECT-Mil treatment components.

Table 2.3
Baseline Clinical Status Categories of Service Members Enrolled in RESPECT-Mil

Construct/Measure	Definition
Depression prominent	One of the following conditions is met: • Probable diagnosis of depression only (see Appendix C); no probable PTSD diagnosis • Minor depression or mild major depression only • (PHQ-9 total score = 10–14) • Moderately severe or severe major depression only (PHQ-9 total score > 15).
PTSD prominent	One of the following conditions is met: • Probable diagnosis of PTSD only (see Appendix E); no probable depression diagnosis • Mild PTSD only (PCL total score = 13–32) • Moderate or severe PTSD only (PCL total score > 33).
DEP+PTSD	One of the following conditions is met: • Probable diagnosis of depression and PTSD • Mild, moderate, or severe depression (PHQ-9 > 10) and mild, moderate, or severe PTSD (PCL total score > 13).

Table 2.4
Constructs and Definitions for RCF Contact Indicators

Construct/Measure	Definition
No RCF contact	A RESPECT-Mil referral was made but no RCF contact was established or recorded.
RCF first contact	RESPECT-Mil recommends that RCFs establish their first contact with service members within seven to ten days after referral into RESPECT-Mil. FIRST-STEPS reports on whether service members have been contacted by RCFs within 14 days of the initial primary care referral.
RCF follow-up contacts	After the RCF first contact, RESPECT-Mil recommends that RCFs schedule routine follow-up contacts every four weeks. During the follow-up contacts, RCFs review the details of the treatment plan, encourage and support treatment adherence, and readminister the PHQ-9 and/or PCL to monitor treatment response. RCF follow-up contacts do not include the RCF first contact.
Timely RCF follow-up contacts	• Early follow-up means that follow-up contact was made within 24 days or fewer after the last RCF contact. • On-time follow-up means that follow-up contact was made within 25–42 days after the last RCF contact. • Late follow-up means that follow-up contact was made 43 days or more after the last RCF contact.
Follow-up assessment recorded	Administration of the PHQ-9 and/or PCL was recorded during the follow-up contact.
Number of days in the program	This means the total number of days that elapsed between the date of the initial primary care referral and the date of the last recorded clinical assessment.

To What Degree Are Service Members Engaging in Psychotropic Medication?

To monitor psychotropic medication treatment, RCFs administer the following question: "Are you taking or has any primary care provider suggested you take any prescribed medication for depression or PTSD?"[2] Service members who endorse a "yes" response are asked an additional set of questions to track medication adherence. We examine service member responses to the following medication adherence question: "Have you been taking the medication for PTSD or depression as it was prescribed?" Response options are: "Filled and Taking," "Filled Taking Sometimes," "Filled but Not Taking," "Not Filled," and "Unknown." RCFs also record the date that service members start psychotropic medications. To assess service member engagement in psychotropic medication treatment, we examined the following:

- during the RCF first contact, the percentage of service members who reported taking a prescribed medication or that their PCPs suggested that they take a prescribed medication for depression or PTSD (*baseline taking/PCP suggests you take medications*)
- during subsequent RCF follow-up contacts, the percentage of service members who reported taking a prescribed medication or that their PCPs suggested that they take a prescribed medication for depression or PTSD (*ever taking/PCP suggests you take medications*)
- the percentage of service members recorded as having started a psychotropic medication (*ever start medications*)

---

[2]   Whether service members are taking medication or whether any PCP has recommended medication are distinct constructs. However, this study's analyses could not examine these constructs separately given the way the psychotropic medication question is asked in FIRST-STEPS.

- during the RCF first contact, the percentage of service members who, when asked about whether they were taking their prescribed medication for depression or PTSD, endorsed either of the following response options: "Filled and Taking" or "Filled Taking Sometimes" (*baseline medication filled and taking or taking sometimes*)
- during the last RCF follow-up contact, the percentage of service members who, when asked about whether they were taking their prescribed medication for depression or PTSD, endorsed either of the following response options: "Filled and Taking" or "Filled Taking Sometimes" (*last follow-up medication filled and taking or taking sometimes*).[3]

Table 2.5 provides a summary of the constructs and definitions we derived to serve as implementation indicators for service member engagement in psychotropic medication treatment.

To What Degree Are Service Members Engaging in Counseling?

To monitor engagement in counseling, RCFs administer the following question during first and follow-up contacts: "Are you attending or has any primary care provider suggested you attend counseling or therapy?"[4] Among service members who report attending counseling or that a PCP suggested that they attend counseling, the following question is administered regarding counseling adherence: "How often are you attending your counseling appointments?" Response options are as follows: "Attend All," "Almost Always," "Often," "Scheduled Not Started," "Started but Stopped," "Seldom," "Never," and "Unknown." RCFs also record the date that service members start any type of counseling or therapy. To assess service member engagement in counseling, we examined the following:

Table 2.5
Constructs and Definitions for Psychotropic Medication Treatment Implementation Indicators

Construct/Measure	Definition
Baseline taking/PCP suggests you take medications	During the RCF first contact, a "yes" response to the question, "Are you taking or has any primary care provider suggested you take any prescribed medication for depression or PTSD?"
Ever taking/PCP suggests you take medications	During any RCF follow-up contacts, a "yes" response to the question, "Are you taking or has any primary care provider suggested you take any prescribed medication for depression or PTSD?"
Ever start medications	Start date of a psychotropic medication recorded during the RCF first contact or any RCF follow-up visit.
Baseline medication filled and taking or taking sometimes	During the RCF first contact, a "Filled and Taking" or "Filled Taking Sometimes" response to the question, "Have you been taking the medication for PTSD or depression as it was prescribed?"
Last follow-up medication filled and taking or taking sometimes	During any RCF follow-up contacts, a "Filled and Taking" or "Filled Taking Sometimes" response to the question, "Have you been taking the medication for PTSD or depression as it was prescribed?"

---

[3]   Given that there may be medications that are prescribed for use on an as-needed basis (e.g., sleep, panic), we included "Filled and Taking Sometimes" as part of the implementation indicator for psychotropic medication use.

[4]   Whether service members are attending counseling or whether any primary care provider has suggested to service members that they attend counseling are distinct constructs. However, this study's analyses could not examine these constructs separately given the way the counseling engagement question is asked in FIRST-STEPS.

- during the RCF first contact, the percentage of service members who reported that they were attending counseling or that their PCPs suggested that they attend counseling (*baseline attending/PCP suggests you attend counseling*)
- during any subsequent RCF follow-up contacts, the percentage of service members enrolled in RESPECT-Mil who reported that they were attending counseling or that their PCPs suggested that they attend counseling (*ever attending/PCP suggests you attend counseling*)
- the percentage of service members recorded as having started counseling (*ever start counseling*)
- during the RCF first contact visit, the percentage of service members who, when asked how often they were attending their counseling appointments, endorsed one of the following response options: "Attend All," "Almost Always," or "Often" (*baseline counseling attend all, almost always, or often*)
- during the last RCF follow-up contact, the percentage of service members who, when asked how often they were attending their counseling appointments, endorsed one of the following response options: "Attend All," "Almost Always," or "Often" (*last follow-up counseling attend all, almost always, or often*).

Based on the available data, we derived implementation indicators for service member engagement in counseling. See Table 2.6 for a summary of constructs and definitions for counseling implementation indicators.

To What Degree Are Service Members Engaging in Self-Management Goals and Psychoeducation?

To monitor service member engagement in self-management goals, RCFs work with service members to identify one or two self-management goals to work on and track progress during the RCF first contact and follow-up contacts. Using FIRST-STEPS, RCFs record whether service members are working on any of the following self-management goals: spending time with people who can support you, practicing relaxation, engaging in pleasurable physical activity,

Table 2.6
Constructs and Definitions for Counseling Implementation Indicators

Construct/Measure	Definition
Baseline attending/PCP suggests you attend counseling	During the RCF first contact, a "yes" response to the question, "Are you attending or has any primary care provider suggested you attend counseling or therapy?"
Ever attending/PCP suggests you attend counseling	During RCF follow-up contacts, a "yes" response to the question, "Are you attending or has any primary care provider suggested you attend counseling or therapy?"
Ever start counseling	Start date of counseling recorded during the RCF first contact or any RCF follow-up visit.
Baseline counseling attend all, almost always, or often	During the RCF first contact, an "Attend All," "Almost Always," or "Often" response to the question, "How often are you attending your counseling appointments?"
Last follow-up counseling attend all, almost always, or often	During RCF follow-up contacts, an "Attend All," "Almost Always," or "Often" response to the question, "How often are you attending your counseling appointments?"

making time for other pleasurable activities, simple goals and small steps, eating nutritious and balanced meals, and avoiding alcohol.

With respect to psychoeducation, RESPECT-Mil has developed informational pamphlets and worksheets to help educate service members about depression and PTSD. During the RCF first contact and follow-up contacts, engagement in psychoeducation is tracked by asking the following question: "Have you received an educational pamphlet on PTSD and/or depression?" If service members answer "yes," RCFs then follow up with the questions, "Have you read the pamphlet?" and "Have you read the worksheet inside the pamphlet?" RCFs record one of the following response options: "Read Material," "Have but Not Read," "Do Not Have Material," and "Unknown." To assess the degree of service member engagement in self-management goals and psychoeducation, we derived the following implementation indicators:

- the percentage of service members who reported working on at least one self-management goal during the RCF first contact or any RCF follow-up contacts (*self-management goals*)
- the percentage of service members who reported having "read material" during the RCF first contact or any RCF follow-up contacts (*psychoeducation*).

Efficacy

To examine outcomes associated with RESPECT-Mil, we posed the following questions: *What proportion of service members experience improvement in depression and/or PTSD symptoms? What proportion of service members experience improvements in functioning?*

To answer these questions, we assessed symptom changes from clinical assessments (i.e., PHQ-9 and/or PCL) administered during the initial primary care visit (baseline) and during the last RCF contact recorded (last follow-up). We derived efficacy indicators that gauged symptom improvement, treatment response, remission, symptom worsening, changes in rates of probable diagnoses, and functional impairment. With respect to symptom improvement, a five-point change on the PHQ-9 is considered to be indicative of a clinically significant response to depression treatment (Kroenke and Spitzer, 2002). Correspondingly, a five-point change on the PCL has been associated with clinically significant change in response to PTSD treatment (Monson et al., 2006; Schnurr, Friedman, Foy, et al., 2003). The National Center for PTSD recommends using a five-point change on the PCL as an indicator of reliable change and ten-point change as an indicator of clinically meaningful response (U.S. Department of Veterans Affairs, 2012). For treatment response, a 50 percent reduction in symptoms from baseline to follow-up assessment has been commonly applied in previous collaborative care studies (see, e.g., Dietrich et al., 2004; Fortney, Enderle, et al., 2012; Fortney, Pyne, et al., 2007; Hedrick et al., 2003; Unützer et al., 2002). To assess whether symptoms worsen from baseline to follow-up, we examined whether there is a five-point increase in clinical assessment scores. Finally, functional impairment is measured by a question that asks whether depression and/or PTSD symptoms have caused difficulties at work, at home, or with people.

We derived the following indicators to assess RESPECT-Mil treatment outcomes:

- the percentage of cases in which clinical assessment scores improved by five or more points from baseline to last follow-up (*symptom improvement*)
- the percentage of cases in which there was a 50 percent decrease in clinical symptom scores from baseline to last follow-up (*treatment response*)
- the percentage of cases in which remission was achieved by the last follow-up (*remission*)

- the percentage of cases in which clinical assessment scores worsened from baseline to follow-up (*symptoms worsen*)
- rates of probable depression and/or PTSD diagnosis at baseline and last follow-up
- rates of functional impairment at baseline and follow-up.

Table 2.7 provides further information about the constructs and measures derived to serve as indicators of the efficacy of RESPECT-Mil.

Aim 2: Facilitators and Barriers to RESPECT-Mil Implementation

To address aim 2, we spoke with RESPECT-Mil providers (e.g., RCFs, PCPs, BHCs, PCCs) as well as the RMIT. This section describes the method used to identify and select potential participants, as well as the development of the discussion protocols and procedures. We then describe the analytic procedure that was used.

RESPECT-Mil Provider Discussions
Sample
In order to maximize variability in provider perspectives about RESPECT-Mil, we selected eight sites (installations) with maximum variability in their implementation of RESPECT-Mil, amount of time since RESPECT-Mil was introduced at the site, and site characteristics (e.g., size, presence of units with high combat exposure).[5] To obtain a rough estimate of sites' implementation of RESPECT-Mil, we examined quantitative clinic-level data on screening

Table 2.7
Constructs and Definitions for Efficacy Indicators

Construct/Measure	Definition
Symptom improvement	The PHQ-9 or PCL total symptom score decreases by five or more points from baseline to last follow-up.
Treatment response	The PHQ-9 or PCL total symptom score decreases by 50 percent or more from baseline to last follow-up.
Remission	Per RESPECT-Mil guidelines, remission for depression is defined as a PHQ-9 total score that is less than five. For PTSD, remission is defined as a PCL total score that is less than 11.
Symptoms worsen	The PHQ-9 or PCL total symptom score increases by five or more points from baseline to last follow-up.
Probable diagnosis	See Appendix C for scoring criteria for depression. See Appendix E for scoring criteria for PTSD.
Functional impairment	Depression and/or PTSD symptoms endorsed as problems that have made it "somewhat difficult," "very difficult," or "extremely difficult" to carry out work, take care of things at home, or get along with other people.

---

[5]   Originally, we aimed to use FIRST-STEPS data to indicate high and low implementation. However, the time required for study approval and for the FIRST-STEPS data to be provided was much longer than expected. In addition, we sought to schedule discussions with RESPECT-Mil providers quickly, as we anticipated that many would be moving soon (e.g., due to permanent changes of station), which would make it more difficult to contact these individuals. Therefore, we decided to derive implementation indicators from the Monthly Screening and Referral Clinic Report data provided by the RMIT instead.

and referral rates at each site for the period between January 2011 and March 2012. Screening rates consisted of the number of primary care visits screened on the MEDCOM Form 774 divided by the number of total primary care visits. Referral rates consisted of the number of positively screened visits referred to RESPECT-Mil or any other program (e.g., behavioral health services) divided by the number of service members who screened positive for PTSD or depression on the MEDCOM Form 774. We ranked sites according to their screening and referral rates, and those sites with high screening and referral rates relative to the other sites were considered to be *high implementers*. Those with low screening and referral rates relative to the other sites were *low implementers*. Of the 37 sites, 13 had high screening and referral rates, six had low rates, and the remaining 18 had mixed rates with some sites having high screening rates but low referral rates and vice versa. Next, we coded each site according to the time RESPECT-Mil has been in place at the site. For example, sites where RESPECT-Mil had only recently been started were in the *early* phase of implementation, whereas those that were among the first to implement the program were in the *late* phase. Finally, we consulted with the RMIT team to gain an understanding of the demographic and geographic characteristics of each site. For example, some sites have large, well-resourced medical facilities, while others have few medical resources. Some are geographically isolated, while others are close to major urban centers or universities. Some sites primarily serve combat-exposed service members soon after they return from deployment, whereas others are predeployment training locations or installations serving very few combat-exposed service members.

Using these sources of information, we selected eight sites based on their implementation level: four high and four low implementers. Within each implementation group (high and low) we ensured that there was variability in population served (e.g., combat exposure), phase of RESPECT-Mil (i.e., early, mid, and late; the range was seven months to five years), and size (e.g., large MTF). Our final sample of eight sites included seven installations based in the continental United States and one outside the United States.

In order to keep the list of selected sites confidential, we obtained a roster of all RESPECT-Mil staff across all installations from the RMIT, not just those selected for this study. We then began contacting all RESPECT-Mil RCFs, PCCs, and BHCs at the eight selected sites to invite them for telephone discussions. Two RCFs on the roster moved to a different location before the completion of the discussion but were retained in our sample. At the end of discussions with PCCs, RCFs, and BHCs, each respondent was asked to nominate two PCPs from his or her clinic to be invited to participate in the study. To obtain variability in views about RESPECT-Mil, researchers encouraged respondents to nominate one PCP who consistently refers to RESPECT-Mil and another who refers to RESPECT-Mil infrequently.

A total of 35 providers completed discussions (see Table 2.8). This included 26 of 30 eligible RCF, PCC, or BHC providers (87 percent). Four (two RCFs and two PCCs) of the 30 providers refused to participate due to lack of time or being new and unfamiliar to the program. One BHC was no longer employed at the installation and obtained a position at another institution. Twenty-six PCPs were nominated for discussions as well, and nine of these PCPs completed discussions (35 percent). Of the remaining 17 nominated PCPs, three were determined to be ineligible: two had moved to different locations, and one had retired. In addition, one nominee refused to participate, and 13 did not respond after several contact attempts. The final sample of participating providers is shown in Table 2.8.

Table 2.8
Final Number of Each Type of Discussion Participant at Each Site

Type of Participant	Site								Total
	1	2	3	4	5	6	7	8	
RCF	1	2	2	1	1	2	1	1	11
BHC	1	1	1	1	1	1	0	1	7
PCC	0	1	2	1	1	1	1	1	8
PCP	1	0	1	1	2	1	1	2	9
Total	3	4	6	4	5	5	3	5	**35**

Discussion Protocol

The RAND research team developed a stage-by-topic discussion protocol (Ryan et al., 2009) (see Appendixes F, G, H, and I). Open-ended questions were generated within each stage and topic. *Stages* were the initial service member encounter, monitoring service members, and coordination. *Topics* were roles and responsibilities, monitoring, implementation, and facilitators. We also included opening and closing questions that were designed to obtain providers' overall impressions of RESPECT-Mil, as well as the way the military health system addresses behavioral health.

Procedure

Prospective participants were initially contacted via email. The email message provided a brief statement about the purpose of the study, extended an invitation for participation, and explained the voluntary and confidential nature of participation. Some providers responded to this email stating their interest in participating and to schedule the discussion. For those who did not respond, a subsequent phone call was made to ensure receipt of the email, request participation in the study, answer questions about the study, and obtain oral consent. Up to four attempts were made to contact the potential participant. Those unable to be reached were removed from consideration for participation in the study. Those who agreed to participate were scheduled for discussions at a time convenient for their schedules.

All discussions were conducted via telephone. A RAND Ph.D.-level researcher and an accompanying note taker conducted each discussion. Participants were reminded of their voluntary participation and confidentiality, and a second request for verbal consent was made and confirmed before the discussion began. Discussions for RCFs, BHCs, and PCCs were designed to take 60 minutes to complete. At the end of the discussion, RCFs and PCCs were asked to identify potential PCPs who might participate. RAND staff obtained contact information for the PCPs and contacted them via email and phone to request participation in the study according to the same procedures used for RCFs, BHCs, and PCCs. Due to their limited availability, the discussion protocol for PCPs was redesigned to be completed in 15 minutes. All participants were thanked for their participation.

RMIT Member Discussions

Sample

Given their limited number, we sought to speak with all 11 RMIT staff. The RMIT provided us with the names and contact information of potential participants. All 11 RMIT members completed discussions (100 percent response rate).

Discussion Protocol

We developed an adapted stage-by-topic (Ryan et al., 2009) RMIT discussion protocol (see Appendix J) that was similar to the format of the provider discussion protocol. The protocol included two main sections: questions about specific RMIT responsibilities and questions about the roles of others who might support RESPECT-Mil implementation (e.g., RMCs). Within the section on specific RMIT responsibilities, the stages were preparing the practice settings, hiring and staffing, training providers and champions, addressing staff turnover, monitoring implementation, coaching calls, site assessment visits, providing feedback to installations, and providing incentives for implementing RESPECT-Mil. The topics in this section were the following questions: "What is involved in this step?" "Who is responsible for this?" "What is working and not working?" "What can be improved?" "What kind of monitoring process (if any) is in place to track performance?" In the second section, which focused on others who may be involved in supporting RESPECT-Mil implementation, the stages were the levels of leadership: clinic administrators, installation level command, and RMC. The topics were the following questions: "What is the role of this person in supporting the implementation of RESPECT-Mil?" "What is working and not working?" "What can be improved?" We also included opening and closing questions that were designed to elicit overall impressions (e.g., "what factors facilitate or inhibit the functioning of the RMIT?").

Procedure

All procedures were reviewed and approved by RAND's and DCoE's institutional review boards. Potential participants were contacted by email. The email sent to potential participants described the purpose of the discussion and explained that discussions were entirely voluntary and confidential. The email also included a project description and a letter of support from DCoE. RMIT members' email responses confirming participation were considered written consent. Respondents reached via phone provided verbal consent.

At the start of each discussion, a RAND researcher explained the purpose of the project and reminded respondents that discussions were voluntary and confidential, but that their remarks might be identifiable by inference by virtue of their roles or perspectives. Then respondents verbally consented to participate. All RMIT discussions were conducted over the phone and were approximately 60 minutes long. RAND Ph.D.-level researchers led the discussions while a second RAND research team member took notes.

Qualitative Analyses

Following the call, the note taker produced written notes, and the discussion facilitator checked and validated the notes. Any additions or discrepancies were discussed in order to produce a final set of notes agreed on by both the discussion facilitator and the note taker. Quotes were separated and then pile sorted into key themes. More detail about the sorting technique is provided in Appendix L.

Following the pile-sort procedures, we developed an outline of a report that would cover the basic themes that emerged. Within each section, we reexamined the quotes for a particular theme across provider types. In this review, we took into account the source of the quote (individual and site), alignment with the RESPECT-Mil program, and placement within the discussion in order to appropriately understand the quote in context. We then summarized the main idea of the theme and the benefits and challenges within the theme, as well as the variability in opinions that we observed within the theme.

Aim 3: Sustainability of RESPECT-Mil Within the Military Health System

For aim 3, we spoke with key stakeholders within the military health system to gain further insight into factors that may influence the sustainability of RESPECT-Mil. RMIT discussions were also used to address aim 3. In the next sections we describe the sampling methodology, the discussion protocol, and analytical approaches used to accomplish aim 3.

Key Stakeholder Discussions
Sample

To select key stakeholders, we sought to recruit individuals serving in administrative or leadership roles within DoD or the Army. We began by obtaining a list of recommended participants from the director of military health at RAND and from RMIT. The list included personnel from RMCs, the U.S. Army Medical Department, MEDCOM, the Office of the Assistant Secretary of Defense for Health Affairs, and Tricare Management Activity.

We used a snowball sample technique to identify additional key stakeholders. At the end of each discussion, respondents were asked if they would like to confidentially recommend other stakeholders to participate in the key stakeholder discussions. The participation of referred stakeholders was not discussed with other respondents in order to maintain confidentiality. As the discussion selection process went on, respondents increasingly recommended that we speak with key stakeholders with whom we had already spoken. Once we were no longer receiving new key stakeholder nominations, we ended the recruitment of stakeholders. Senior leadership from RAND's military health research group, RMIT, and respondents provided contact information for some key stakeholders. Otherwise, the RAND research team found publicly available stakeholder contact information through online research.

Of the 43 key stakeholders who were contacted, 24 participated (56 percent). Two individuals who were contacted for a discussion directly refused to participate. Seventeen individuals were contacted with the correct email address or phone number but did not respond or follow up in scheduling the requested discussion. Several stakeholders invited others from their organizations to be present during the discussions, resulting in an additional seven stakeholders who took part in the study. In these cases, the discussions were conducted with groups of stakeholders. Thus, in total, 31 stakeholders participated.

Discussion Protocol

The RAND research team developed the discussion protocol (see Appendix K). The stakeholder protocol was designed in an open-ended question format to seek high-level observations about RESPECT-Mil. This allowed respondents to speak to specific components of the processes, program outcomes, and the broad behavioral health setting in the military, depending on their knowledge and viewpoints.

The discussion protocol included five main sections:

1. familiarity with RESPECT-Mil
2. the role of RESPECT-Mil within the respondent's organization
3. positive and negative aspects of RESPECT-Mil
4. RESPECT-Mil compared with other initiatives (e.g., PCMH)
5. suggestions for improvement and recommendations.

Procedure

All procedures were reviewed and approved by the RAND Human Subjects Protection Committee and by DCoE. Potential participants were contacted by email first. A follow-up email was sent if we received no response from the initial email. If there was no response after these two emails, we called the stakeholder to inquire about a discussion. We stopped contacting stakeholders who had not responded to two emails and two telephone calls.

The email sent to potential participants described the purpose of the discussion and explained that discussions were entirely voluntary and confidential. The email also included a project description and a letter of support from DCoE. Stakeholders' email responses confirming participation were considered written consent. Respondents reached via phone provided verbal consent.

At the start of each discussion, a RAND researcher explained the purpose of the project and reminded respondents that discussions were voluntary and confidential, but that their remarks might be identifiable by inference by virtue of their roles or perspectives. Then respondents verbally consented to participate. All stakeholder discussions were conducted over the phone and were approximately 60 minutes long. RAND Ph.D.-level researchers led the stakeholder discussions while a second RAND researcher took notes.

Qualitative Analyses

The analytic procedures used in aim 2 were similarly employed for aim 3. The same pile-sort procedure was applied to the key stakeholder discussion (see the qualitative analyses section for aim 2). However, the new set of themes was developed without relying on the themes identified in the provider discussions.

CHAPTER THREE

RESPECT-Mil Implementation: Findings from Monthly Screening and Referral Clinic Reports and FIRST-STEPS

As described in Chapter Two, we developed RESPECT-Mil implementation indicators based on the RE-AIM framework (Glasgow, Vogt, and Boles, 1999). Using data from the Monthly Screening and Referral Clinic Reports and FIRST-STEPS, we describe the degree to which RESPECT-Mil is being implemented along the following RE-AIM dimensions: reach, adoption, implementation fidelity, and efficacy. When possible, we compare our results with findings from other depression and PTSD collaborative studies. This runs counter to the standard practice of presenting findings from other studies in a subsequent discussion section. However, given the lack of standardized benchmarks for quality implementation of collaborative care programs, we viewed this comparison as important for interpreting this study's findings. It should be noted that other depression and PTSD collaborative care studies differ from one another and from RESPECT-Mil on a number of dimensions. Collaborative care studies vary with respect to the clinical assessments used to screen and track depression or PTSD symptoms (e.g., PHQ-9 versus the Symptom Checklist–20 [SCL-20]), intervention components (e.g., medication management, cognitive behavioral therapy), intervention intensity (e.g., number of sessions, treatment duration), the criteria employed to measure treatment outcomes (e.g., 40 percent versus 50 percent reduction in symptoms), and the organizational settings in which the program is being implemented (e.g., health maintenance organization, community-based organization), and the scope of the implementation effort (e.g., number of sites and clinics). In addition, as will be discussed in Chapters Four and Five, implementing collaborative care within the military health service system may pose unique challenges (e.g., deployments, staff turnover) that should be taken into consideration when interpreting findings. Findings from other collaborative care studies are intended to provide a broad frame of reference when considering RESPECT-Mil implementation findings. Tables 3.1 and 3.2 provide a summary of PTSD and depression collaborative care studies that we reference to assist with the interpretation of the RESPECT-Mil implementation findings.

Reach

To assess reach, we examined the degree to which RESPECT-Mil is enhancing the detection of unmet mental health needs among service members as well as the extent to which referrals are being made to facilitate access to care. Using screening and referral data submitted by 84 Army primary care clinics, we report on the outcome of 647,642 primary care visits made during the period from August 2011 to March 2012. Figure 3.1 provides a flow diagram illustrating the outcome of these primary care visits using the reach implementation indicators. The definitions for the reach indicators are provided in Table 2.2 in Chapter Two.

Table 3.1
PTSD Collaborative Care Studies

	Study Design	Setting	No. of Sites	No. of Clinics	No. of Patients Enrolled in Treatment	Intervention Components
Coordinated Anxiety Learning and Management (CALM) (Craske et al., 2011)	RCT	Civilian	4	17	33	Computerized cognitive behavioral therapy with anxiety clinical specialist and medications.
RESPECT-PTSD (Schnurr, Friedman, Oxman, et al., 2013)	RCT	VA medical center	4	5	96	Telephone support calls from care managers (doctoral-level psychologists) to promote treatment adherence.
Stepped collaborative care (Zatzick et al., 2004)	RCT	Trauma center	1	1	60	Six months of case management delivered by a trauma center clinical specialist, followed by cognitive behavioral therapy, motivational interviewing, and/or medications if symptoms persist.

NOTE: RCT = randomized controlled trial

Table 3.2
Depression Collaborative Care Studies

	Study Design	Setting	No. of Sites	No. of Clinics	No. of Patients Enrolled In Treatment	Intervention Components
Translating Initiatives for Depression into Effective Solutions (TIDES) (Chaney et al., 2011)	Cluster RCT	VA primary care clinics	5	7	386	Treatment options included watchful waiting, medication, and referral to cognitive behavioral therapy. Care managers (nurses) provide follow-up, assessment, and support for medication adherence and side effects.
RESPECT-D (Dietrich, 2004)	Cluster RCT	Health care organizations	5	60	224	Care manager support for treatment adherence and self-management practice. Care manager assessment and follow-up contacts.
Telemedicine Enhanced Antidepressant Management (TEAM) (Fortney, Pyne, Edlund, et al., 2007)	Cluster RCT	VA community-based outpatient clinics	1	3	189	Stepped care. Telephone support from the care manager (nurse) to assess clinical symptoms, educate and activate, and address treatment barriers. If there is no response to medications, the pharmacist conducts a medication history, provides pharmacotherapy recommendations to PCPs, and nonscripted medication management over the phone to patients.

Table 3.2—Continued

	Study Design	Setting	No. of Sites	No. of Clinics	No. of Patients Enrolled In Treatment	Intervention Components
Telemedicine-Based Collaborative Care (Fortney, Enderle, et al., 2012)	Nonrandomized implementation evaluation	VA community-based outpatient clinics	3	11	298	Care management telephone support, which included education/activation, barrier assessment/resolution, symptom monitoring, medication adherence monitoring, side-effects monitoring, and self-management. No formal guidelines for referrals to specialty mental health.
Collaborative Care Depression Treatment VA Primary Care (Hedrick et al., 2003)	Cluster RCT	Primary care	1	2	177	Telephone support from care managers (social workers) to encourage adherence, address treatment barriers, and assess treatment response. Treatment options include antidepressant medication, adjunctive medication, a cognitive behavioral therapy group, schedule with psychologist or psychiatrist (referral to mental health specialist). Least resource-intensive options were selected first; more intensive treatment options provided if no response at six or 12 weeks.
Improving Mood-Promoting Access to Collaborative Treatment (IMPACT) (Unützer et al., 2002; Hegel et al., 2005; Chan, Fan, and Unützer, 2011)	RCT	Civilian and VA health care organizations (five states)	8	18	906	Care managers (nurses or psychologists) provide psychoeducation, problem-solving therapy (six to eight sessions), and medication.
Partners in Care (Wells, Sherbourne, Schoenbaum, et al., 2000)	Cluster RCT	Health managed care organizations	6	27	443	Quality-improvement model. Institutional commitment (practices agreed to reserve in-kind resources up to one-half of estimated costs of implementing interventions and time costs for study participation). Care managers (nurses) assess, educate, and activate patients to support treatment adherence. Individual or group cognitive behavioral therapy available.

Figure 3.1
Screening and Referral Clinic Data from August 2011 to March 2012

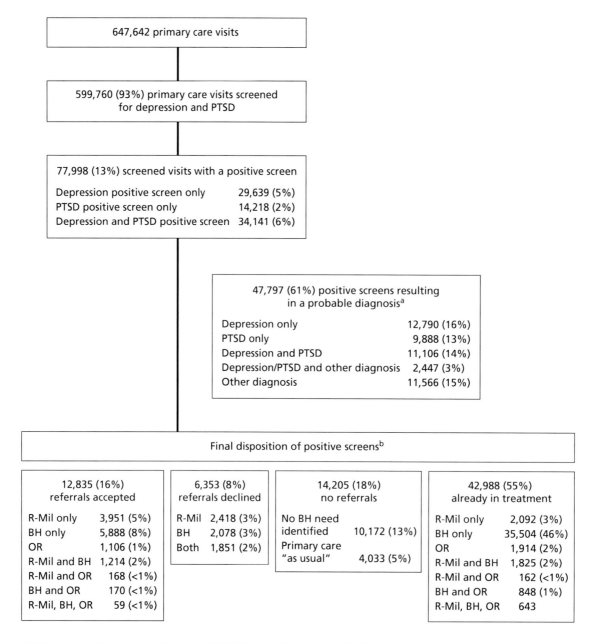

647,642 primary care visits

599,760 (93%) primary care visits screened
for depression and PTSD

77,998 (13%) screened visits with a positive screen

Depression positive screen only	29,639 (5%)
PTSD positive screen only	14,218 (2%)
Depression and PTSD positive screen	34,141 (6%)

47,797 (61%) positive screens resulting
in a probable diagnosis[a]

Depression only	12,790 (16%)
PTSD only	9,888 (13%)
Depression and PTSD	11,106 (14%)
Depression/PTSD and other diagnosis	2,447 (3%)
Other diagnosis	11,566 (15%)

Final disposition of positive screens[b]

12,835 (16%)
referrals accepted

R-Mil only	3,951 (5%)
BH only	5,888 (8%)
OR	1,106 (1%)
R-Mil and BH	1,214 (2%)
R-Mil and OR	168 (<1%)
BH and OR	170 (<1%)
R-Mil, BH, OR	59 (<1%)

6,353 (8%)
referrals declined

R-Mil	2,418 (3%)
BH	2,078 (3%)
Both	1,851 (2%)

14,205 (18%)
no referrals

No BH need identified	10,172 (13%)
Primary care "as usual"	4,033 (5%)

42,988 (55%)
already in treatment

R-Mil only	2,092 (3%)
BH only	35,504 (46%)
OR	1,914 (2%)
R-Mil and BH	1,825 (2%)
R-Mil and OR	162 (<1%)
BH and OR	848 (1%)
R-Mil, BH, OR	643

[a]Of the total visits screened, 8 percent (47,797) resulted in a probable diagnosis.
[b]The final dispositions of 1,617 (2 percent) of the positive screens were unknown due to missing data.
NOTES: R-Mil = RESPECT-Mil; BH = behavioral health; OR = other psychosocial resource.
RAND *RR588-3.1*

To What Extent Does RESPECT-Mil Facilitate the Identification of Service Members with Mental Health Needs Related to Depression and/or PTSD?

Visits Screened and Positive Screens

Among the U.S. Army primary care clinics that have implemented RESPECT-Mil, 93 percent (or 599,760) of the visits made during the eight-month period from August 2011 to March 2012 were screened for PTSD and depression. Of all screened visits, 13 percent (77,998) had a positive screen (see Figure 3.1). More specifically, 5 percent (29,639 visits) had a positive screen for depression only, 2 percent (14,218 visits) had a positive screen for PTSD only, and 6 percent (34,141 visits) had a positive screen for depression and PTSD.

The Post-Deployment Health Assessment (PDHA) employs the same PHQ-2 depression and PC-PTSD brief screening items that RESPECT-Mil administers via the MEDCOM Form 774. In a study conducted with U.S. Army service members from one infantry brigade combat team undergoing the routine PDHA, rates of positive screens for PTSD and depression were two to three times greater when administered anonymously (7.7 percent with PTSD; 7 percent with depression; 12 percent with PTSD and depression) than in a simultaneous nonanonymous PDHA (3.3 percent with PTSD; 1.9 percent with depression; 4.2 percent with PTSD and depression) (Warner et al., 2011).

Concerns regarding the underreporting of PTSD and depression by service members have been well documented (Institute of Medicine, 2012). The degree to which underreporting may be occurring with RESPECT-Mil primary care screening is unknown. RESPECT-Mil differs from other screening and collaborative care studies on numerous dimensions, making it difficult to compare screening rates. For instance, although RESPECT-Mil and PDHA both use the PHQ-2 as their depression screeners, they employ different response options and criteria for a positive screen. In addition, screening rates found for the PDHA as well as for other studies are provided at the individual level as opposed to the RESPECT-Mil screening and referral data, which are based on individual primary care visits. Moreover, the prevalence rates of depression and PTSD can vary across the settings and populations in which collaborative care studies are conducted. Nonetheless, findings indicate that at an absolute level, a considerable number of service members are reporting depression and PTSD symptoms, as evidenced by the number of positive screens resulting from routine screening in the Army's primary care settings. During the eight-month period, from August 2011 to March 2012, nearly 80,000 service members endorsed depression and/or PTSD symptoms when completing the brief screeners.

Positive Screens Resulting in a Probable Diagnosis

Screened visits resulting in a positive screen are immediately followed up with a clinical interview and self-administered clinical assessments (e.g., PHQ-9, PCL) to determine probable diagnosis. Sixty-one percent (47,797) of the positive screens resulted in a probable diagnosis of a mental health disorder (see Figure 3.1). Forty-six percent (36,231) of the positive screens resulted in a probable diagnosis of PTSD, depression, or both. Another 15 percent (11,566) of positive screens resulted in a diagnosis other than PTSD or depression. With respect to the total proportion of visits screened (not shown in Figure 3.1), 6 percent of all screened visits resulted in a probable diagnosis of PTSD and/or depression, while another 2 percent of screened visits resulted in the identification of some other mental health disorder diagnosis.

To What Degree Does RESPECT-Mil Support Referrals to Needed Mental Health Treatment?

To determine the extent to which RESPECT-Mil is connecting service members to needed mental health treatment, we examined the final disposition of visits with positive screens (see Figure 3.1).

Of the total positive screens, 16 percent (12,835) resulted in a referral being accepted to one or more sources of mental health treatment. As seen in Figure 3.1, when accounting for accepted referrals across one or more sources of care, approximately 8 percent of positively screened visits resulted in an accepted referral to RESPECT-Mil, 10 percent led to an accepted referral to behavioral health, and 2 percent accepted a referral to some other psychosocial resource.

With respect to referrals declined, approximately 8 percent of positively screened visits had been referred to RESPECT-Mil and/or behavioral health but were declined. Further, no referrals were issued for 18 percent of positive screens because either no behavioral health treatment need was identified (13 percent) or the case was addressed in primary care as usual without the enhanced support of RESPECT-Mil (5 percent). Another 55 percent of positive screens had been documented as already being followed in treatment. Of the positive screens that were documented as already being followed in treatment, the largest group of cases (46 percent, 35,504) were being cared for by behavioral health only. Approximately 6 percent of positive screens were already being followed in RESPECT-Mil. Findings are consistent with a study conducted with the VA population in which approximately half of primary care patients who had a positive screen for depressive symptoms were already being treated for mental health issues within the VA health care system (Rubenstein, Chaney, and Smith, 2004). Altogether, no referral had been issued among 73 percent of positive screens due to service members already being in treatment, no behavioral health treatment need being identified, or treatment being designated to primary care.

Overall, in reference to the reach of RESPECT-Mil, findings indicate that at an absolute level, RESPECT-Mil is identifying a substantial number of service members who are reporting depression and PTSD symptoms, as evidenced by the number of positive screens resulting from routine screening. Moreover, a substantial proportion of positive screens are resulting in the detection of not only probable diagnoses of depression and PTSD but also other mental diagnoses. Of the total positive screens, only a smaller proportion (13 percent) was identified as not having any behavioral health need. Of the 19,188 referrals provided (referrals accepted plus referrals declined), approximately two-thirds of the referrals were accepted, resulting in a sizeable number of service members being connected to needed mental health care. More than half of the positive screens flagged service members who were already in treatment but appeared to continue to experience clinical symptoms. To the extent that routine screenings can facilitate additional support for service members who are already in treatment but are not experiencing symptom improvement, this may be another venue in which RESPECT-Mil can address unmet mental health needs.

Adoption

To gauge the degree to which RESPECT-Mil is being adopted across the 37 Army installations, we examined the extent to which sites were reaching service members with mental health needs (see Table 2.2 for definitions of reach indicators). For each of the individual installations, we examined the screening and referral patterns for depression and PTSD. More-detailed information is provided in the following sections. The range of implementation months ranged from three to 64 months. At the time of the study, ten sites had been implementing RESPECT-Mil for 12 months or fewer, 11 sites between 13 and 24 months, six sites between 25 and 48 months, and eight sites for 50 months or more. This reflects the phased rollout of RESPECT-Mil, with some sites having implemented the program for several months and others for a number of years.

How Do Installations Vary with Respect to the Identification and Referral of Service Members with Mental Health Needs?

Visits Screened, Positive Screens, and Probable Depression and/or PTSD Diagnosis

With respect to the implementation of routine screening for depression and PTSD, a majority of installations (25 of the 37) were screening a high proportion of visits, with a range of 91 percent to 99 percent of visits screened (see Figure 3.2). Thirty-one of the 37 installations were screening at least 80 percent of their visits. The proportion of screened visits that resulted in a positive screen also varied across installations, with a range of 4 percent to 24 percent. Similarly, the degree to which positive screens resulted in a probable depression or PTSD diagnosis differed across sites (a range of 11 percent to 100 percent). Finally, the percentage of screened visits resulting in a probable depression and/or PTSD diagnosis ranged from 1 percent to 17 percent. Overall, a large proportion of primary care visits across sites had been screened for depression and PTSD, irrespective of the length of time implementing RESPECT-Mil. Exceptions included two sites that screened fewer than half of their primary care visits even though they had been implementing RESPECT-Mil for four years or longer. Thus, a longer duration of program implementation did not necessarily ensure higher screening rates.

Figure 3.2
Visits Screened, Positive Screens, and Probable Depression and/or PTSD Diagnosis

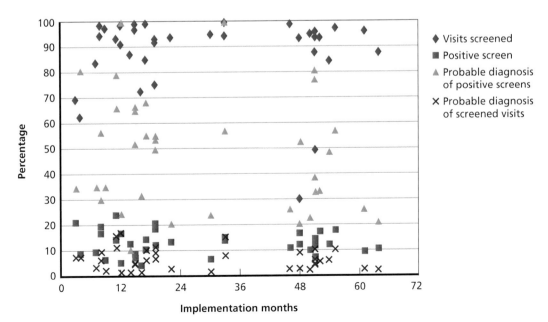

Rates of positive screens were also fairly uniform across sites, with varying lengths of time implementing RESPECT-Mil. In contrast, rates of probable diagnosis resulting from positive screens were more variable, with no evident or consistent relationship to the length of implementation. The factors underlying the variation in rates of probable diagnosis are unknown and could be due to a host of reasons, such as site differences in the clinical presentation of service members, service member willingness to disclose symptoms, and provider administration of clinical assessments.

Referrals Accepted

Figure 3.3 provides a breakdown of the percentage of positive screens resulting in an accepted referral to RESPECT-Mil, behavioral health, or another psychosocial resource across the 37 installations. Rates of accepted referrals to RESPECT-Mil versus behavioral health fluctuated across installations, with some sites yielding comparable rates across the two resources and other sites tending to facilitate referrals to one resource over the other. Rates of accepted referrals to other psychosocial resources appeared to be lower compared with RESPECT-Mil and behavioral health. With respect to the proportion of positive screens that resulted in an accepted referral to any source of care, ten of the 37 installations had referral rates that were 20 percent or greater and 24 of the 37 installations had referral rates that ranged from 10 percent to 19 percent.

Referrals Declined

Figure 3.4 presents the percentage of positive screens that resulted in referrals being declined across the 37 installations. Of the positive screens, only five of 37 installations sites had rates of declined referrals to RESPECT-Mil that were 10 percent or greater. Only three of the 37

Figure 3.3
Percentage of Positive Screens Resulting in Referrals Accepted to RESPECT-Mil, Behavioral Health, or Another Psychosocial Resource

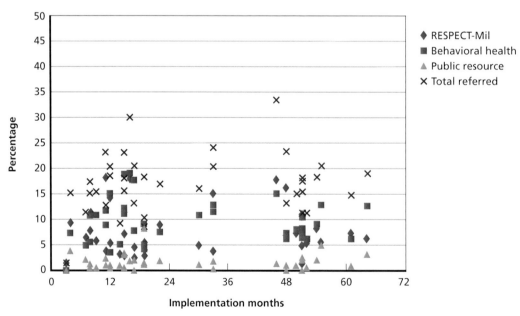

Figure 3.4
Percentage of Positive Screens Resulting in Referrals Declined to RESPECT-Mil and Behavioral Health

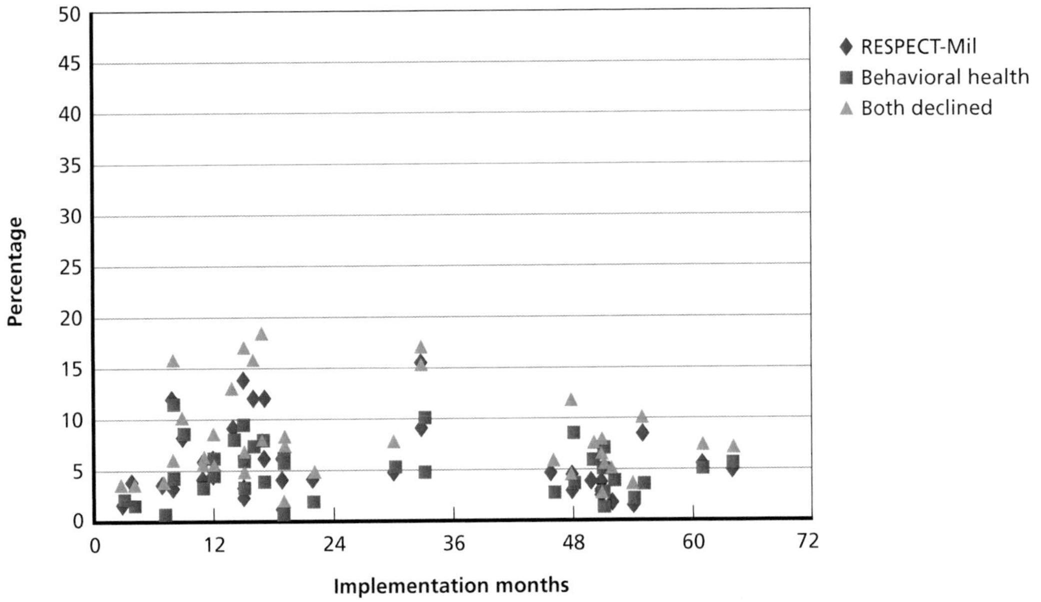

installations sites had rates of declined referrals for behavioral health that were 10 percent or greater. Eleven of the 37 installations had rates of declined referrals that were greater for RESPECT-Mil than behavioral health. In contrast, for 15 of the 37 installations, rates of declined referrals were greater for behavioral health than RESPECT-Mil. However, for several of the installations, the differences in declined referrals between the two sources were slight. For nine of the 37 installations, the difference in rates of declined referrals between the two sources was twice as high or greater.

No Referral Made

As shown in Figure 3.5, installations varied with respect to the proportion of positive screens for which no referrals were provided—either because no behavioral treatment need was identified or because the behavioral health need was addressed in primary care. For 19 of the 37 installations, there were relatively low proportions of positive screens (less than 10 percent) that resulted in no behavioral treatment need being identified. For three installations, approximately a third of positive screens resulted in no behavioral treatment need being identified. For the remaining 15 installations, no behavioral treatment need was identified for 10 percent to 24 percent of the positive screens. Across installations, a much smaller proportion of positive screens resulted in no referral being made because the presenting behavioral health need wound up being addressed in primary care. For 33 of the 37 installations, less than 10 percent of the positive screens resulted in the behavioral health need being addressed in primary care. For the remaining four installations, between 10 percent and 15 percent of positive screens ended up being directed to primary care.

Figure 3.5
Percentage of Positive Screens Resulting in a Behavioral Health Need Not Being Identified or a Behavioral Health Need Being Addressed in Primary Care

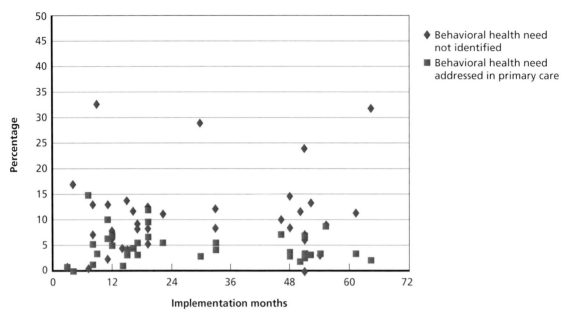

Already Enrolled in Treatment

Figure 3.6 provides estimates on the percentage of positive screens of service members who were documented as already being in treatment. For eight of the 37 installations, approximately 10 percent or more of the positive screens were of service members who were already enrolled in RESPECT-Mil. For the majority of installations (20 of 37), 50 percent or more of the positive screens were associated with service members who reported already receiving care in behavioral health. Across installations, the percentage of positive screens that resulted in capturing service members who were already receiving treatment in behavioral health was much greater than those already receiving treatment from RESPECT-Mil or from another public resource. With respect to the percentage of positive screens for service members who were already receiving *any* type of treatment, the range was 35 percent to 77 percent across installations.

In sum, the large majority of sites had adopted routine screening for depression and PTSD during primary care visits. Moreover, the rates of identified mental health needs with respect to positive screens were rather consistent across sites. Rates of probable diagnoses and referrals were more variable across sites, but there was no clear relationship between duration of program implementation and these adoption indicators. The extent to which variations in probable diagnoses and referral rates are due to service member factors (e.g., differences in clinical symptoms, willingness to disclose, preferences for certain types of services) versus provider factors (e.g., administration of clinical assessments, willingness to address mental health needs) is unknown.

Figure 3.6
Percentage of Positive Screens Who Were Already Enrolled in RESPECT-Mil, Behavioral Health, or Another Psychosocial Resource

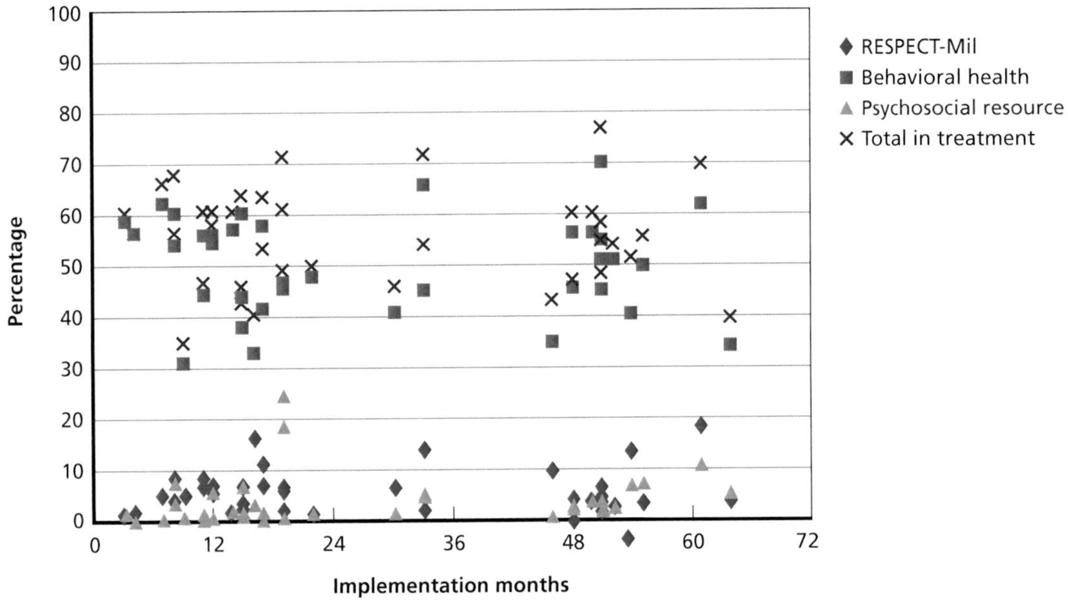

Implementation

To assess how key components of RESPECT-Mil are being implemented, we analyzed clinical assessment and treatment monitoring information recorded by RCFs in the FIRST-STEPS database on the 3,403 service members who had been enrolled in the program from August 2011 to March 2012. Service members had to have started treatment and had their cases closed during this period or had to have been enrolled in the program for at least six months. Implementation fidelity was examined by looking at the recorded course of treatment for this set of service members. We first looked at the recorded clinical presentation of service members enrolled into RESPECT-Mil, the degree and nature of RCF contacts, and service member engagement in treatment. Figure 3.7 provides a summary and flow diagram of the detailed implementation analyses that follow. It is important to note that data presented in this section reflect only the information recorded by RCFs in FIRST-STEPS. Other activities may have occurred that were not recorded, and thus cannot be described here.

To What Degree Is RESPECT-Mil Enrolling Service Members with Depression and/or PTSD?

For the purpose of this study, the baseline clinical status of service members was classified according to the following categories: depression prominent, PTSD prominent, or DEP+PTSD (see Table 2.3 in Chapter Two). The baseline clinical status categories are employed throughout the implementation and efficacy analyses. These clinical status categories were derived so that comparisons could be made with other depression and PTSD collaborative care studies,

Figure 3.7
Flow Diagram of Implementation and Efficacy Analyses (August 2011–March 2012)

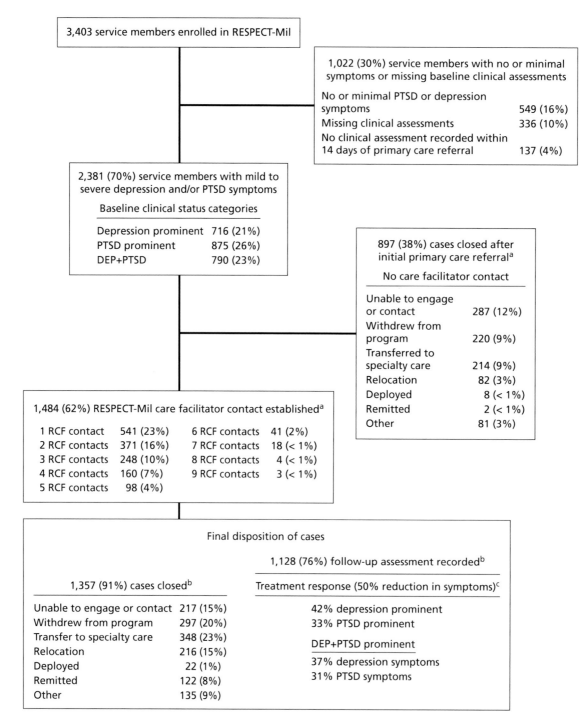

[a] Percentages are of the 2,381 service members with mild to severe symptoms.
[b] Percentages are of the 1,484 service members who had established contact with RCFs.
[c] Percentages are of the 1,128 service members with a follow-up assessment recorded.

which, in contrast to RESPECT-Mil, have focused exclusively on the treatment of depression *or* PTSD.[1]

Of the 3,403 service members enrolled in RESPECT-Mil, 30 percent had no or minimal symptoms or were missing clinical assessments (see Figure 3.7). Specifically, 16 percent of service members enrolled in RESPECT-Mil had no or minimal clinical symptoms (i.e., a PHQ-9 score of less than 10 and/or a PCL score of less than 13), 10 percent had no clinical assessments recorded, and 4 percent had no clinical assessments recorded within 14 days of the initial primary care referral. As such, these cases were not classified according to the baseline clinical status categories and were not included in the main implementation analyses. However, at the end of the main implementation analyses, we include a section describing the course of treatment among service members with no or minimal depression and/or PTSD symptoms.

The remaining 70 percent of service members enrolled in RESPECT-Mil were classified according to one of the baseline clinical status categories (see Figure 3.7). Within each of the baseline clinical status categories, we provide a breakdown of the symptom severity levels of service members. Symptom severity levels are based on the definitions provided by RESPECT-Mil (see Appendixes C and E). Percentages are of the total sample of service members enrolled in RESPECT-Mil.

Among service members enrolled in RESPECT-Mil, 21 percent (716) were classified as depression prominent. We provide a breakdown of the percentage of service members enrolled in RESPECT-Mil across the different depression-prominent clinical-symptom severity levels:

- 13.0 percent (*N* = 442) probable depression only (no probable PTSD diagnosis)
- 7.1 percent (*N* = 243) minor depression or mild major depression only (a PHQ-9 score of 10–14)
- 0.9 percent (*N* = 31) moderately severe or severe major depression only (a PHQ-9 score greater than or equal to 15).

Of those enrolled in RESPECT-Mil, 26 percent (875) of service members were classified as PTSD prominent. The breakdown of the percentage of service members enrolled in RESPECT-Mil across the PTSD-prominent clinical symptom is as follows:

- 12.7 percent (*N* = 432) probable PTSD only (no probable depression diagnosis)
- 11.9 percent (*N* = 404) mild PTSD only (a PCL score of 13–32)
- 1.2 percent (*N* = 39) moderate or severe PTSD only (a PCL score greater than or equal to 33).

Twenty-three percent (790) of service members enrolled in RESPECT-Mil were classified under the DEP+PTSD baseline clinical status category. Of service members enrolled in RESPECT-Mil, the percentage breakdown across the severity levels of the depression and PTSD clinical symptom is as follows:

---

[1]   The degree to which RESPECT-Mil is enrolling service members with clinical need could be considered an indicator of reach. However, for ease of presentation, the clinical status categories are presented in the implementation fidelity section so that the process of care can be tracked from enrollment to final disposition. Clinical status categories were also included within the implementation fidelity section given that the degree to which clinical assessments were administered and recorded in FIRST-STEPS was considered an aspect of implementation fidelity

- 18.0 percent (N = 613) probable depression and PTSD
- 5.2 percent (N = 177) mild or moderate depression (a PHQ-9 score greater than 10) and PTSD (a PCL greater than 13).

Findings indicate that service members who are being enrolled in RESPECT-Mil are presenting with a variety of clinical issues and a wide range of clinical symptom severity levels. Service members who are enrolling in RESPECT-Mil do not appear to be disproportionately representing one type of mental disorder over another. With respect to prominent presenting clinical symptoms, service members are being enrolled for depression only, PTSD only, and depression and PTSD symptoms at comparable rates. A greater proportion of service members who presented with depression and PTSD symptoms met criteria for a probable diagnosis (18 percent of RESPECT-Mil enrollees) compared with service members who presented with depression symptoms alone (13 percent of RESPECT-Mil enrollees) or PTSD symptoms only (12.7 percent of RESPECT-Mil enrollees). Almost a quarter of service members enrolled in RESPECT-Mil had depression and/or PTSD symptoms that were in the mild to moderate range. Subthreshold levels of depression and/or PTSD have been shown to be associated with comparable levels of functional impairment and have been shown to respond to collaborative care treatment (Grubaugh et al., 2005; Judd et al., 1996; Wells, Sherbourne, Duan, et al., 2005).

Among the 1,055 service members with a probable depression diagnosis (442 depression prominent diagnoses plus 613 DEP+PTSD diagnoses), 42 percent had a comorbid probable PTSD diagnosis. Other collaborative care studies conducted with depressed primary care patients have yielded lower rates of comorbid PTSD (Campbell et al., 2007; Chan, Fan, and Unützer, 2011; Fortney, Pyne, Edlund, et al., 2007). Collaborative care studies conducted with depressed veterans in the VA have found rates of comorbid probable PTSD that range from 24 percent using a clinical diagnostic interview (Fortney, Pyne, Edlund, et al., 2007) to 36 percent using a brief PTSD screen (Campbell et al., 2007). Among an older civilian primary care population with depression, a much smaller proportion of patients (11 percent) had comorbid probable PTSD according to a brief screen (Chan, Fan, and Unützer, 2011).

Among the 1,045 service members with a probable diagnosis of PTSD (432 PTSD prominent diagnoses plus 613 DEP+PTSD diagnoses), 41 percent had a comorbid probable depression diagnosis. Higher rates of comorbid depression have been found in other PTSD collaborative care studies. Among VA primary care patients with PTSD, 67 percent (treatment condition) to 73 percent (treatment as usual) had comorbid probable depression according to PHQ-9 assessments (Schnurr, Friedman, Oxman, et al., 2013). Among civilian primary care patients with PTSD, 86 percent (treatment as usual) to 88 percent (treatment condition) had comorbid depression according to a clinical diagnostic interview (Craske et al., 2011).

In contrast to other depression and PTSD collaborative care studies, RESPECT-Mil enrolled service members who presented with no or minimal depression or PTSD symptoms. According to baseline PHQ-9 and PCL scores, 16 percent of service members had no or minimal symptoms. The reasons for enrolling service members who had no or minimal depression or PTSD symptoms are unknown. It is possible that service members may have been presenting with other behavioral health needs unrelated to depression or PTSD. In addition, there may have been service members who were apprehensive about endorsing depression or PTSD symptoms on formal clinical assessments, but during the course of the initial primary care visit, providers may have perceived behavioral health needs. A small percentage of service members who had no or minimal symptoms at baseline did meet criteria for probable depression and/or PTSD diagnosis at follow-up. More-detailed information about the process of care for these service members is provided at the end of the implementation section. Finally, 10 percent of service members had no clinical assessments recorded. The clinical presentation and symptom severity level of these service members are unknown. The baseline clinical presentation of another 4 percent of service members also could not be determined, given that no clinical assessments were recorded within the 14 days of the initial primary care referral.

To What Extent Are RCFs Able to Implement Their RESPECT-Mil Responsibilities?

Table 2.4 in Chapter Two lists the set of implementation indicators used to assess the degree and nature of RCF contacts. The following set of analyses is restricted to the 2,381 service members who had mild to severe levels of depression and/or PTSD symptoms. RCF contact with service members with no or minimal symptoms are presented separately in a subsequent section, given that RESPECT-Mil guidelines recommend a less intensive course of treatment (see Appendixes C and E).

No RCF Contact

Ensuring a successful handoff from the PCP to the RCF is an integral component of RESPECT-Mil. Of the 2,381 service members with mild to severe depression and/or PTSD symptoms, 38 percent (897) never established contact with an RCF and had their cases closed after the initial primary care referral. The reasons for case closure after the initial primary care referral are presented in Figure 3.7. Twelve percent of service members with mild to severe PTSD and/or depression had their cases closed after the initial primary care referral because RCFs were unable to engage or contact service members, and another 9 percent withdrew from the program. An additional 9 percent of service members were transferred to specialty care. The remaining service members whose cases were closed before establishing contact with an RCF were recorded as having deployed (less than 1 percent), remitted (less than 1 percent), or left the program for an unspecified reason.

Table 3.3 presents the same information on the percentage of cases closed after the initial primary care referral and the reasons for closure across the baseline clinical status categories. Among service members classified as depression prominent, 35 percent (252) had their cases closed after the initial primary care referral and never established contact with an RCF. Among depression prominent service members, 13 percent (90) had their cases closed because RCFs were unable to engage or contact service members, 8 percent (61) withdrew from treatment, 7 percent (51) were transferred to specialty care, 3 percent (19) had relocated, less than 1 percent (3) had deployed or remitted, and 4 percent (27) had left RESPECT-Mil for some unspecified reason. The rates of case closures after the initial primary care referral appear to be comparable across the baseline clinical status categories. More than a third of depression prominent (35 percent), PTSD prominent (38 percent), and DEP+PTSD (39 percent) service members had their cases closed after the initial primary care referral before establishing contact with an RCF. Correspondingly, the reasons for case closure seem to be similarly distributed across the three clinical groups, with a large proportion of cases closed because of an inability to contact or engage service members or because service members withdrew from the program.

The proportion of service members who were enrolled in RESPECT-Mil but did not make contact with an RCF is in the middle range compared with other similar collaborative care studies. For depression collaborative care studies, the proportion of patients who never

Table 3.3
Percentage of Cases Closed After Initial Primary Care Referral and Reason for Case Closure

Baseline Clinical Status	Case Closed After Referral		Unable to Engage/ Contact		Withdrew		Transferred to Specialty Care		Relocated		Deployed		Remitted		Other	
	N	%	N	%	N	%	N	%	N	%	N	%	N	%	N	%
Depression (N = 716)	252	35	90	13	61	8	51	7	19	3	2	<1	1	<1	27	4
PTSD (N = 875)	334	38	104	12	92	10	76	9	30	3	5	<1	0	0	26	3
DEP+PTSD (N = 790)	311	39	93	12	67	8	87	11	33	4	1	<1	1	<1	28	4
TOTAL (N = 2,381)	897	38	287	12	220	9	214	9	82	3	8	<1	2	<1	81	3

NOTE: For DEP+PTSD, depression and PTSD symptoms were present at baseline.

establish contact with a care facilitator has extended from a low of 2 percent (Unützer et al., 2002) and 3 percent (Fortney, Pyne, Edlund, et al., 2007) to a midrange of 27 percent (Wells, Sherbourne, Schoenbaum, et al., 2000) and 44 percent (Chaney et al., 2011), to a high range of 91 percent (Fortney, Endele, et al., 2012). John Fortney and his coauthors (2012) found that only 9 percent of patients who were diagnosed with depression during the primary care visit had an encounter with the care manager.[2] However, rates varied across clinics, with a range of 1 percent to 49 percent of patients diagnosed with depression who had no contact with the care manager. Moreover, even though 84 PCPs had made depression diagnoses, only 69 percent (58 out of 84 PCPs) had referred at least one patient to the care manager. Thus, in contrast to RESPECT-Mil, the high proportion of patients who had not established contact with a care manager appeared to be due in part to the lack of PCP referrals. With respect to a similar collaborative care study for PTSD in the VA, 11 percent of veterans never made contact with the care facilitator (Schnurr, Friedman, Oxman et al., 2013). In a recent metaanalytic review of depression collaborative care programs, reluctance to enroll in collaborative care programs was identified as a barrier to implementation (Thota et al., 2012). In this current evaluation of RESPECT-Mil, we were unable to determine the extent to which difficulties in establishing contact with service members were due to a reluctance to engage in the program or insufficient efforts by RCFs to reach out to service members.

RCF First Contact and Follow-Up Contacts

As seen in Figure 3.7, 62 percent (1,484) of service members with mild to severe depression and/or PTSD symptoms had established contact with an RCF. Among service members with mild to severe clinical symptoms, 23 percent had one RCF contact, 16 percent had two RCF contacts, 10 percent had three RCF contacts, 7 percent had four RCF contacts, 4 percent had five RCF contacts, and approximately 4 percent had six or more RCF contacts. Thus, 23 percent of service members enrolled in RESPECT-Mil had only an RCF first contact and no additional RCF follow-up contacts. Thirty-nine percent of service members enrolled in RESPECT-Mil had one or more RCF follow-up contacts. This is lower than the rate found in the RESPECT-D study, in which 64 percent of depressed primary care patients had one or more follow-up phone calls with a care facilitator within the first three months of treatment (Dietrich et al., 2004).

Table 3.4 provides information about the extent to which the RCF first contact was established within 14 days of the initial primary care referral, mean number of RCF follow-up contacts, mean number of days between RCF follow-up contacts, and the mean number of days service members were enrolled in the program. Among service members who had established contact with an RCF, 60 percent had their first RCF contact recorded within 14 days of the initial primary care referral. After the first RCF contact, service members had on average 2.6 follow-up RCF contacts. The mean number of days between follow-up visits was 36. With respect to the duration of treatment, service members were enrolled in RESPECT-Mil for an average of 56.7 days. The mean number of RCF follow-up contacts and treatment duration fall slightly below RESPECT-Mil's recommended guidelines. As specified by the RESPECT-

---

[2] It is important keep in mind the differences across these collaborative care studies when comparing findings. For instance, unlike most collaborative care studies, which are designed as RCTs, the Fortney, Sherbourne, Schoenbaum, et al. (2012) study is a nonrandomized evaluation of the effectiveness of evidence-based quality improvement strategies to implement collaborative care management of depression in VA satellite clinics.

Table 3.4
RCF First Contact, Follow-Up Contacts, and Days in RESPECT-Mil

Baseline Clinical Status	Among Service Members Who Established Contact with an RCF							
	RCF First Contact Within 14 Days of Referral		Number of RCF Follow-Up Contacts		Number of Days Between Follow-Up Contacts		Number of Days in Program	
	N	%	M	SD	M	SD	M	SD
Depression (N = 464)	292	63	2.5	1.6	34	14.5	69	54.6
PTSD (N = 541)	318	59	2.7	1.6	37	16.8	78	58.1
DEP+PTSD (N = 479)	282	59	2.5	1.5	37	17.5	71	56.7
TOTAL (N = 1,484)	892	60	2.6	1.6	36	16.4	73	56.7

NOTE: M = mean; SD = standard deviation. For DEP+PTSD, depression and PTSD symptoms were present at baseline. Follow-up contacts do not include the RCF first contact.

Mil guidelines, the acute phase of treatment typically occurs within the first four months of treatment, during which there are monthly follow-up RCF contacts. During the acute phases of treatment, the RCF first contact should occur within 14 days of the initial referral, and a total of four follow-up RCF contacts should be made. In a collaborative care depression study with older civilian primary care patients, the mean number of care facilitator contacts was 16 among patients with depression and among patients with comorbid depression and PTSD over the course of a 12-month treatment period (Hegel et al., 2005). Low attendance at appointments has been identified as an implementation barrier in several studies (Thota et al., 2012).

Table 3.5 presents analyses on all follow-up contacts recorded by RCFs. We report the percentage of all follow-up contacts in which a clinical assessment was recorded and the percentage of follow-up contacts that were conducted on time. Nearly 80 percent of all RCF follow-

Table 3.5
Follow-Up Assessment Conducted, Number of Total Follow-Up Contacts, and Timely Follow-Up Contacts

Baseline Clinical Status	Among Service Members Who Established Contact with an RCF								
	Total Number of Follow-Up Contacts	Total Follow-Up Contact Assessments Recorded		Timeliness of Follow-Up Contacts					
				Early		On Time		After	
	N	N	%	N	%	N	%	N	%
Depression (N = 464)	714	644	90	169	24	397	56	148	21
PTSD (N = 541)	911	822	90	165	18	552	61	194	21
DEP+PTSD (N = 479)	708	641	91	147	21	404	57	157	22
Total (N = 1,484)	2,333	2,107	90	481	21	1,353	58	499	21

NOTE: For DEP+PTSD, depression and PTSD symptoms were present at baseline.

up contacts were either early (within 24 days of prior contact) or on time (within 25 to 42 days of prior contact). The proportion of timely follow-up visits is relatively high compared with a similar depression collaborative care implementation VA study in which 43 percent of the follow-up visits were on time during the acute phases of treatment (Fortney, Sherbourne, Schoenbaum, et al., 2012). In addition, a clinical assessment was conducted for 90 percent of the follow-up contacts that were recorded. To the extent that contacts of shorter duration (e.g., very brief telephone check-ins) or contacts that did not include clinical assessments were not always recorded in the database, these data may undercount actual contacts between RCFs and service members. These data only reflect follow-up contacts in which the questions in the FIRST-STEPS module or clinical assessments were administered and recorded in FIRST-STEPS.

In sum, RCFs were able to implement certain RESPECT-Mil responsibilities more readily than others. As in other collaborative care studies, RCFs experienced challenges establishing contact with a substantial proportion of service members after the initial primary care referral to RESPECT-Mil. Moreover, RCFs were unable to engage service numbers in the recommended number of follow-up contacts. Of the RCF follow-up contacts that were made, a high proportion of the follow-up contacts had been conducted on time and had included clinical assessments to track treatment responses. Service members remained enrolled in RESPECT-Mil on average for approximately two months, which is a shorter time frame than outlined by the program.

Are Service Members Participating in the Full Course of Recommended Treatment?

To assess treatment engagement, we investigated RESPECT-Mil service members' involvement in psychotropic medication, counseling, psychoeducation, and self-management goals as documented and recorded by RCFs within FIRST-STEPS. According to RESPECT-Mil protocol, during the RCF first contact and follow-up contacts, RCFs administer a series of questions to monitor psychotropic medication use and adherence, counseling use and adherence, engagement in self-management goals, and the receipt of psychoeducation. In addition, RCFs track the start date and status changes in psychotropic medication use and counseling.

To What Degree Are Service Members Engaging in Psychotropic Medication?

Table 3.6 provides data on psychotropic medication use. At baseline (i.e., RCF first contact), 9 percent of service members reported either currently taking psychotropic medication or that their PCPs had suggested that they take psychotropic medication.[3] This increased to 53 percent by the last follow-up contact. In addition, according to psychotropic medication logs in FIRST-STEPS, 39 percent of service members reported starting medications while enrolled in RESPECT-Mil. These findings suggest that psychotropic medication use and PCP recommendations for psychotropic medication increased over the course of enrollment in RESPECT-Mil. Service members classified as DEP+PTSD reported slightly greater levels of psychotropic medication use and PCP recommendations for psychotropic medication use. Among service members who had been prescribed a medication, medication adherence appeared to be somewhat consistent from baseline (60 percent) to last follow-up contact (61 percent), with records

---

[3]   Whether service members are taking medication or whether any PCP has suggested to service members that they take medication are distinct constructs. However, this study's analyses could not examine these constructs separately given the way the medication engagement question is asked in FIRST-STEPS.

Table 3.6
Service Members Taking or PCP Suggesting Medications, Ever Start Medications, and Medication Adherence

	Among Service Members Who Established Contact with an RCF									
Baseline Prominent Symptoms	Baseline Taking/ PCP Suggests You Take Medications		Ever Taking/PCP Suggests You Take Medications		Ever Start Medications		Baseline Filled and Taking or Taking Sometimes[a]		Last Follow-Up Filled and Taking or Taking Sometimes*	
	N	%	N	%	N	%	N	%	N	%
Depression (N = 464)	37	8	233	50	178	38	22/37	60	19/37	51
PTSD (N = 541)	40	7	265	49	198	37	31/40	78	25/40	63
DEP+PTSD (N = 479)	60	13	285	60	210	44	29/60	48	40/60	67
TOTAL (N = 1,484)	137	9	783	53	586	39	82/137	60	84/137	61

NOTE: For DEP+PTSD, depression and PTSD symptoms were present at baseline.

[a] Questions administered only to service members who reported taking medication or that a PCP suggested medication use.

indicating that service members had filled and were taking their medications at least sometimes. From baseline to last follow-up contact, rates of medication adherence appeared to decrease among depression prominent and PTSD prominent service members, but the rate increased among DEP+PTSD service members.

Service members' use of psychotropic medication was relatively lower than rates found in other collaborative care studies. Depression collaborative care studies conducted in the VA have found rates of psychotropic medication use that have ranged from 73 percent (Fortney, Pyne, Edlund, et al., 2007) to 80 percent (Hedrick et al., 2003). Among older civilian depressed patients in primary care, 62 percent reported taking psychotropic medication at the three-month follow-up (Unützer et al., 2002). In the RESPECT-D study, 88 percent of patients reported taking antidepressants at the three-month follow-up (Dietrich et al., 2004). In the RESPECT conducted with VA primary care patients with PTSD, 83 percent reported taking psychotropic medications (Schnurr, Friedman, Oxman, et al., 2013). Finally, in a stepped care collaborative study conducted with trauma care patients, 34 percent were offered pharmacotherapy, but only half of these patients reported taking the psychotropic medication (Zatzick et al., 2004).

To What Degree Are Service Members Engaging in Counseling?

At baseline, only 14 percent of service members reported either attending counseling or that their PCPs suggested that they attend counseling.[4] By the last RCF follow-up contact, this increased to 67 percent (see Table 3.7). Based on counseling data in FIRST-STEPS, 23 percent of service members were recorded as having started counseling while enrolled in RESPECT-

---

[4]   Whether service members are attending counseling or whether any PCP has suggested to service members that they attend counseling are distinct constructs. However, this study's analyses could not examine these constructs separately given the way the counseling engagement question is asked in FIRST-STEPS.

Table 3.7
Attend Counseling or PCP Suggesting Counseling, Ever Start Counseling, and Adherence

Baseline Prominent Symptoms	Among Service Members Who Established Contact with an RCF									
	Baseline Attending/PCP Suggests You Attend Counseling		Ever Attending/ PCP Suggests You Attend Counseling		Ever Start Counseling		Baseline Attend All/Almost Always/Often*		Last Follow-Up Attend All/Almost Always/Often*	
	N	%	N	%	N	%	N	%	N	%
Depression (N = 464)	59	13	295	64	95	20	17/59	29	26/59	44
PTSD (N = 541)	61	11	344	64	128	24	19/61	31	32/61	52
DEP+PTSD (N = 479)	81	17	350	73	120	25	26/81	32	41/81	51
TOTAL (N = 1,484)	201	14	989	67	343	23	62/201	31	99/201	49

NOTE: For DEP+PTSD, depression and PTSD symptoms were present at baseline.

* Questions administered only to service members who reported attending counseling or PCP suggesting attending counseling.

Mil. Among service members who obtained counseling, findings indicate that counseling adherence increased over the course of enrollment in RESPECT-Mil. Among service members who reported obtaining counseling, rates of adherence (defined by attending all counseling sessions, almost always, or often) increased from baseline (31 percent) to the last follow-up contact (49 percent).

Comparable rates of engagement in counseling were found in the RESPECT-D study, in which 26 percent of patients reported receiving counseling within the first three months of treatment (Dietrich et al., 2004). Depression collaborative studies in the VA had counseling engagement rates that ranged from 22 percent (Hedrick et al., 2003) to 43 percent (Fortney, Pyne, Edlund et al., 2007). In the RESPECT study, 55 percent of VA primary care patients with PTSD reported having a psychotherapy visit (Schnurr, Friedman, Oxman, et al., 2013).

Table 3.8 presents information on the extent to which service members who had established contact with RCFs had ever started medications or counseling, worked on a self-management goal, or read psychoeducational materials while enrolled in RESPECT-Mil. Rates of engagement in medication or counseling, self-management goals, and psychoeducation appeared comparable across the three baseline clinical status categories. Overall, 46 percent of service members were recorded as having started either psychotropic medication or counseling while enrolled in RESPECT-Mil.

To What Degree Are Service Members Engaging in Self-Management Goals and Psychoeducation?

According to the RESPECT-Mil protocol, RCFs are to identify one to two self-management goals that service members are working on and review progress during RCF contacts. Self-management goals could include practicing relaxation, engaging in a pleasurable physical activity, making time for other pleasurable activities, eating nutritious meals, and avoiding alcohol. More than half of service members (67 percent) were recorded as having worked on a self-management goal. The rate of engagement in self-management goals appears to be much

Table 3.8
Ever Start Medication or Counseling, Self-Management, and Psychoeducation

Baseline Prominent Symptoms	Among Service Members who Established Contact with an RCF					
	Ever Start Medication and/or Counseling		Working on Self-Management Goal		Read Psychoeducational Materials	
	N	%	N	%	N	%
Depression (N = 464)	202	44	311	67	265	57
PTSD (N = 541)	245	45	374	69	343	63
DEP+PTSD (N = 479)	236	49	315	66	289	60
TOTAL (N = 1,484)	683	46	1,000	67	897	60

NOTE: For DEP+PTSD, depression and PTSD symptoms were present at baseline.

greater than found in a VA quality improvement study on the implementation of collaborative care for depression in which self-management goals were discussed in only 15 percent of the total follow-up contacts (Fortney, Enderle, et al., 2012). In RESPECT-Mil, among depression prominent service members, 49 percent of the total follow-up contacts involved addressing a self-management goal, whereas 53 percent and 52 percent of the total follow-up contacts involved a self-management goal for PTSD prominent and DEP+PTSD service members, respectively (data not shown).

RESPECT-Mil psychoeducational pamphlets and worksheets have been developed to help educate service members about depression and PTSD. Approximately 60 percent of service members were recorded as having read the psychoeducational materials. This figure is relatively low compared with the Fortney, Enderle, et al. (2012) study, in which rates of overall reach were lower, but among those who were reached, psychoeducation was provided during 100 percent of the care manager contact visits. Comparable rates of psychoeducation were found in RESPECT-D, which used a lower threshold to index the provision of psychoeducation. Among individuals with a care manager contact, 71 percent were offered psychoeducational materials (Dietrich et al., 2004).

Summary of Treatment Engagement Findings

Overall, 46 percent of service members had started either psychotropic medication or counseling while enrolled in RESPECT-Mil. Although PCP recommendations for psychotropic medication and service member initiation of psychotropic medications appeared to increase over the course of RESPECT-Mil, only 39 percent of service members had started psychotropic medications, which is relatively lower than rates found in other collaborative care studies. Similarly, rates of attending counseling or having a PCP recommend counseling increased during the course of being enrolled in RESPECT-Mil. In total, 23 percent of service members were recorded as having started counseling while enrolled in RESPECT-Mil, which is comparable to some other collaborative care studies (Dietrich et al., 2004; Hedrick et al., 2003). The relatively low overall rate of engagement in psychotropic medication or counseling may be due to the fact that a substantial proportion of service members only had a single RCF contact. Of the 1,484 service members who had established contact with an RCF, 36 percent (541) had their initial contacts but no follow-up contacts. Follow-up contacts may have been critical in facilitating the uptake of such treatments, especially given the low percentage of service members who were currently engaged in or had providers suggesting medications or counseling at initial contact. More than 60 percent of service members were recorded as having engaged in self-management goals and in psychoeducation, which is comparable to or higher than rates found in other collaborative care studies.

Efficacy

What Proportion of Service Members Experience Improvement in Depression and/or PTSD Symptoms?

To ascertain outcomes associated with RESPECT-Mil, we used FIRST-STEPS data to investigate clinical outcomes across depression prominent, PTSD prominent, and DEP+PTSD service members who had at least one clinical assessment recorded in an RCF follow-up contact (see Table 3.9). Among depression prominent service members, 75 percent (350) had a PHQ-9 follow-up assessment recorded. Among PTSD prominent service members, 74 percent (403) had a PCL follow-up assessment recorded. Among DEP+PTSD service members, 78 percent (375) had a PHQ-9 follow-up assessment and 73 percent (348) had a PCL follow-up assessment recorded. To measure a service member's response to treatment, we examined symptom changes from the baseline clinical assessment to the last follow-up assessment recorded. With respect to symptom improvement, nearly half of depression prominent service members demonstrated a clinically significant response to treatment from baseline to follow-up assessment. Among PTSD prominent service members, a comparable proportion, 53 percent, exhibited reliable symptom change. Among DEP+PTSD service members, 39 percent experienced clinically significant change in depression symptoms, and 60 percent demonstrated reliable clinical change in PTSD symptoms.

Regarding treatment response, 42 percent of depression prominent service members experienced a 50 percent reduction in depression symptoms from baseline to the last follow-up assessment. PTSD prominent service members demonstrated lower rates of treatment response, with only 33 percent demonstrating similar decreases in symptoms. DEP+PTSD

Table 3.9
Symptom Improvement, Treatment Response, Remission, and Symptoms Worsening

| Baseline Prominent Symptoms | Among Service Members with a Follow-Up Assessment Recorded | | | | | | | | | |
| | Follow-Up Assessment Recorded | | Symptom Improvement (≥ 5 points) | | Treatment Response (50% Decrease) | | Remission (PHQ-9 < 5) (PCL < 11) | | Symptoms Worsen (≥ 5 points) | |
	N	%	N	%	N	%	N	%	N	%
Depression (N = 464)	350	75	163/350	47	147/350	42	101/350	29	0/350	0
PTSD (N = 541)	403	74	215/403	53	131/403	33	105/403	26	83/403	21
DEP+PTSD (N = 479)										
Depression	375	78	148/375	39	140/375	37	82/375	22	0/375	0
PTSD	348	73	210/348	60	107/348	31	65/348	19	47/348	14

NOTE: For DEP+PTSD, depression and PTSD symptoms were present at baseline.

service members had slightly lower rates of treatment response for depression (37 percent) and PTSD (31 percent). The rate of treatment response among depression prominent service members is comparable to the VA quality improvement collaborative care implementation study, which yielded a 34 percent treatment response rate using the same PHQ-9 assessment (Fortney, Enderle, et al., 2012). Other collaborative studies have employed the SCL-20 (Derogatis, Lipman, and Covi, 1973) to measure responses to depression treatment. At the three-month follow-up, which is similar to the mean duration of treatment in RESPECT-Mil, a 17 percent treatment response rate was found among VA patients (Hedrick et al., 2003), a 30 percent treatment response was found among older primary care patients with depression symptoms only (Unützer et al., 2002), and a 53 percent treatment response was found among civilian primary care patients in the RESPECT-D study (Dietrich et al., 2004). Another VA depression collaborative care study yielded a treatment response rate of 24 percent at the six-month follow-up (Fortney, Pyne, Edlund, et al., 2007). In a civilian collaborative care study for anxiety disorders, a 50 percent treatment response rate was found at six-month follow-up, but this was while using a less stringent criterion (i.e., a 40 percent reduction in PCL scores) (Craske et al., 2011).

As defined by RESPECT-Mil guidelines, the remission of symptoms is a PHQ-9 total score below 5 for depression and a PCL below 11 for PTSD. Remission rates among depression prominent service members (29 percent) rates were somewhat similar to PTSD prominent service members (26 percent). Among DEP+PTSD service members, remission rates were slightly lower for depression (22 percent) and PTSD (19 percent). The remission rate for service members presenting predominantly with depression was comparable to the VA depression collaborative care implementation study, which also had a 29 percent remission rate using the PHQ-9 with a slightly more-stringent criteria (i.e., symptom free) (Fortney, Enderle, et al., 2012). Other depression collaborative care studies have reported remission rates at three-month follow-up that have ranged from 26 percent (Dietrich et al., 2004) to 30 percent (Unützer et al., 2002) using different criteria (i.e., SCL-20 score below 0.05). At the six-month follow-up, these studies yielded higher remission rates, which ranged from 37 percent (Dietrich et al., 2004) to 49 percent (Unützer et al., 2002). PTSD remission rates for PTSD prominent and DEP+PTSD service members in RESPECT-Mil were substantially higher than rates found in the analogous RESPECT-PTSD study conducted with VA patients (Schnurr, Friedman, Oxman, et al., 2013). In RESPECT-PTSD, at the six-month follow-up, remission rates were 8 percent for patients who received high-fidelity care, 6 percent for patients who received low-fidelity care, and 9 percent for patients who received no 3CM care.

None of the service members enrolled in RESPECT-Mil experienced a worsening of depression symptoms by five or more points. In contrast, 21 percent of PTSD prominent and 14 percent of DEP+PTSD service members had PCL scores that increased by five or more points from baseline to the follow-up assessment. Based on the combined estimates of service members presenting with either PTSD or DEP+PTSD prominent symptoms, this means that slightly more than one in six service members experienced an aggravation of PTSD symptoms while in treatment. Findings suggest that service members presenting with PTSD should be carefully monitored for potential worsening of symptoms. Further investigation is warranted to assess whether observed deteriorations in treatment are related to service members not engaging in the full recommended course of treatment or whether a referral to behavioral health may be indicated for more intractable PTSD symptoms.

Table 3.10 displays the rates of probable depression, PTSD, and functional impairment at baseline and the last follow-up assessment.[5] Among depression prominent service members with a follow-up assessment recorded, the proportion of those who had a probable depression diagnosis decreased by more than half from baseline (65 percent) to the last assessment (27 percent). Among PTSD prominent service members, the proportion who had a PTSD probable diagnosis also decreased from baseline (47 percent) to the last follow-up assessment (31 percent). Similar to the depression prominent service members, rates of probable depression diagnoses among DEP+PTSD service members decreased by nearly half from baseline (75 percent) to the last follow-up assessment (38 percent). However, compared with PTSD prominent service members, a greater proportion of DEP+PTSD service members met the probable PTSD diagnosis at baseline (77 percent), and the decrease in percentage of service members who had probable PTSD at last follow-up assessment (48 percent) was greater.

Rates of probable depression diagnoses among service members during their last follow-up assessments were in the midrange compared with rates found in other depression collaborative care studies. However, rates of probable depression diagnoses from other collaborative care studies were assessed at a longer follow-up period (i.e., six-month follow-up) and with patients who may have had a longer duration of treatment (e.g., up to 12 months). At the six-month follow-ups, rates of probable depression diagnoses ranged from 22 percent in the IMPACT study (Unützer et al., 2002) using the Structured Clinical Interview diagnostic (First et al., 1997) to 55 percent in the Partners in Care study (Wells, Sherbourne, Schoenbaum, et al., 2000) using the Center for Epidemiologic Studies Depression Scale (Radloff, 1977). Rates of probable PTSD diagnosis at follow-up among service members enrolled in RESPECT-Mil were comparable to findings from another PTSD collaborative care study. In the stepped col-

Table 3.10
Probable Diagnosis and Functional Impairment at Baseline and Last Follow-Up Assessment

Baseline Prominent Symptoms	Among Service Members with a Follow-Up Assessment Recorded									
	Baseline Probable Diagnosis		Last Follow-Up Probable Diagnosis		Change in Percentage Points	Baseline Functional Impairment		Last Follow-Up Functional Impairment		Change in Percentage Points
	N	%	N	%		N	%	N	%	
Depression (N = 350)	226	65	96	27	27	331	95	235	67	28
PTSD (N = 403)	189	47	126	31	16	349	87	274	68	19
DEP+PTSD										
Depression (N = 375)	284	76	141	38	37	359	96	287	77	19
PTSD (N = 348)	268	77	167	48	29	332	95	270	78	17

NOTE: For DEP+PTSD, depression and PTSD symptoms were present at baseline.

---

[5]   To facilitate comparisons with other PTSD studies, the means and standard deviations for the baseline and last follow-up PCL scores are provided in Appendix M. For comparability, the PCL response options were recoded from one to five.

laborative care PTSD study, rates of probable PTSD diagnoses ranged from 24 percent at the three-month follow-up to 22 percent at the six-month follow-up (Zatzick et al., 2004).

What Proportion of Service Members Show Improvement in Functioning?

As seen in Table 3.10, a large majority of service members was recorded as experiencing functional impairment related to depression and/or PTSD clinical symptoms at the baseline assessment. Among depression prominent service members, only 5 percent reported no functional impairment, which increased sixfold at the last follow-up assessment, with 33 percent reporting no functional impairment associated with depression symptoms. A similar reduction in functional impairment was found among DEP+PTSD service members, with 5 percent reporting no depression-related functional impairment at baseline, which increased to 22 percent at the last follow-up assessment. Among PTSD prominent service members, 13 percent reported no functional impairment at baseline, which increased to 32 percent at the last follow-up assessment. In contrast, among DEP+PTSD service members, a smaller proportion reported at baseline no PTSD-related functional impairment (5 percent), which increased fourfold at the last follow-up assessment, with 22 percent reporting no PTSD-related functional impairment.

Final Disposition of Cases

Among the 1,484 service members who had established contact with an RCF, 91 percent (1,357) had their cases closed, as recorded in the FIRST-STEPS database. Reasons for closure, which were recorded by RCFs, are shown in Figure 3.7. Although only 8 percent of service members who had contact with an RCF were coded as having achieved remission (122 of 1,484), the actual remission rates are likely to be much greater based on estimates from the last follow-up assessment scores. Table 3.9 provides data on service members who had achieved remission based on the last follow-up clinical assessment. Among service members who had a follow-up assessment recorded, nearly a third (101) of depression prominent service members and approximately a fifth (105) of PTSD prominent service members had achieved remission. Among DEP+PTSD service members with a follow-up assessment recorded, 22 percent (83) achieved remission from depression and 19 percent (66) attained remission from PTSD. The discrepancy in the number of service members recorded as having achieved remission based on the last follow-up clinical assessment versus case closure categories may be due to recording or data entry errors. Further, among service members who had established contact with an RCF, another 15 percent of cases were closed due to an inability to engage or contact service members; additionally, 20 percent withdrew from the program, 23 percent were transferred to specialty care, and 15 percent relocated.

Overall, rates of treatment response and remission were within the range of other collaborative care studies. Of the service members with depression prominent symptoms, 42 percent exhibited a treatment response (i.e., a 50 percent reduction in symptoms) compared with rates of 17 percent (Hedrick et al., 2003) to 53 percent (Dietrich et al., 2004) found in other depression collaborative care studies. Of the service members with PTSD prominent symptoms, 33 percent had demonstrated a treatment response, which is somewhat comparable to the only other collaborative care study with PTSD patients that reported rates of treatment response. Michelle Craske and coauthors (2011) reported a 50 percent treatment response rate, but this was with a longer follow-up period (six months) and a less stringent criterion (i.e., a 40 percent reduction in symptoms).

Similarly, 29 percent of service members with depression prominent symptoms in RESPECT-Mil reached remission, which is within the range of other depression collaborative care studies, which reported rates of 26 percent (Dietrich et al., 2004) to 30 percent (Unützer et al., 2002). Of the service members with PTSD symptoms in RESPECT-Mil, 26 percent had reached remission at the last follow-up, which is substantially greater than that found in a similar collaborative care program for PTSD for veterans. In Paula Schnurr and her coauthors' RESPECT-PTSD study (2013), 8 percent of veterans in high-fidelity care and 6 percent in low-fidelity care reached remission at the end of a comparatively longer six-month follow-up period. Note, the RESPECT-PTSD study enrolled veterans who met diagnostic criteria for PTSD and thus may have had participants with greater clinical symptom severity than RESPECT-Mil. Finally, approximately 20 percent of PTSD prominent and DEP+PTSD service members reported at the last follow-up assessment no longer experiencing functional impairment related to their clinical symptoms. A slightly larger proportion of depression prominent service members (28 percent) reported at the last follow-up assessment no longer experiencing functional impairment.

Though the clinical outcomes evidenced in RESPECT-Mil appear to be comparable to other studies, our evaluation did not employ an RCT design, given that the program had already been implemented throughout Army installations before the start of the evaluation. Hence, our evaluation cannot address how the RESPECT-Mil program fares compared with treatment as usual. Systematic reviews indicate that collaborative care programs yield significant improvements in depression and anxiety outcomes (Archer et al., 2012; Gilbody et al., 2006; Thota et al., 2012). However, less extensive research has been conducted with primary care collaborative care interventions for PTSD. Only two RCT studies have been published that were conducted on primary care collaborative care programs for the treatment of PTSD. In the CALM study, although there was a smaller subset of participants with PTSD, the effect size for the treatment group was comparable to that found for the other treated anxiety disorders (i.e., generalized anxiety disorder, panic disorder, social anxiety disorder), which demonstrated superior outcomes to treatment as usual (Craske et al., 2011). In the RESPECT-PTSD study, no differences in PTSD symptoms or functioning were found between the treatment and usual care participants (Schnurr, Friedman, Oxman, et al., 2013). However, participants who were assigned to collaborative care were more likely to have made a mental health visit and to fill an antidepressant prescription than participants assigned to usual care.

Service Members with No or Minimal Clinical Symptoms

Although service members with no or minimal clinical symptoms were not the primary focus of the implementation analyses, we provide a summary of their course of treatment as recorded in FIRST-STEPS. Of the 549 service members who had no or minimal clinical symptoms among those enrolled in RESPECT-Mil, 43 percent had their cases closed after the initial primary care referral without ever having established contact with an RCF. See Figure 3.8 for the breakdown of the reasons for case closure (i.e., no RCF contacts). Further, 23 percent of service members with no or minimal clinical symptoms had one RCF contact, 14 percent had two RCF contacts, 10 percent had three RCF contacts, 5 percent had four RCF contacts, and 5 percent had five or more RCF contacts. The degree of RCF contacts among service members with no or minimal clinical symptoms appears to be comparable to service members with mild to severe clinical symptoms (see Figure 3.8).

Among service members who had established contact with an RCF, 32 percent were recorded as having started medications, 15 percent started counseling, 64 percent were working on self-management goals, and 54 percent had read psychoeducational materials. At baseline, 8 percent of service members reported taking medication or that their PCPs suggested that they take medications, which increased to 44 percent during the course of being enrolled in RESPECT-Mil. Correspondingly, 10 percent of service members reported attending counseling or that their PCPs suggested that they attend counseling, which increased to 54 percent during the tenure of RESPECT-Mil enrollment. On average, service members were enrolled in RESPECT-Mil for 65 days.

Among those who had established contact with an RCF, 59 percent (186) had a follow-up PHQ-9 recorded (depression assessment) and 16 percent (46) a follow-up PCL recorded (PTSD assessment). Two percent of service members with no or minimal baseline clinical symptoms (11 of 549) met criteria for probable depression at the last follow-up clinical assessment. One percent of service members with no or minimal baseline clinical symptoms (six of 549) met criteria for probable PTSD at the last follow-up clinical assessment. Among service members who had made contact with an RCF, the majority (94 percent) had their cases closed within the time period of the FIRST-STEPS data used for this study. See Figure 3.8 for the breakdown of the reasons for case closure.

Findings suggest that service members who were enrolled in RESPECT-Mil with no or minimal clinical symptoms were engaging in similar levels of treatment compared with service members with mild to severe depression and PTSD symptoms. Implementation indicators for service members with mild to severe clinical symptoms are presented in Tables 2.3 through 2.5 in Chapter Two. The proportion of service members who established contact with an RCF, the number of RCF contacts, and engagement in medication, counseling, self-management goals, and psychoeducation were nearly equivalent across the two groups. It is unclear whether these service members were experiencing other types of mental distress that were not captured by the baseline clinical assessments. It is possible that during the clinical interviews, PCPs may have detected mental health issues that warranted monitoring and referral into RESPECT-Mil. Alternatively, some PCPs may be administering the clinical assessment and referral procedures improperly. Another explanation could be that service members were reluctant to endorse symptoms on clinical assessments that might be documented within their medical records. A small proportion of service members who presented with no or minimal symptoms at baseline met criteria for probable depression or PTSD at the last follow-up assessment. This could be evidence of service members' hesitation to acknowledge symptoms at baseline but being more willing during the course of treatment to admit to symptoms. Alternatively, it is also possible that service members experienced a worsening of their symptoms during the course of treatment.

Figure 3.8
Service Members with No or Minimal Depression and PTSD Symptoms

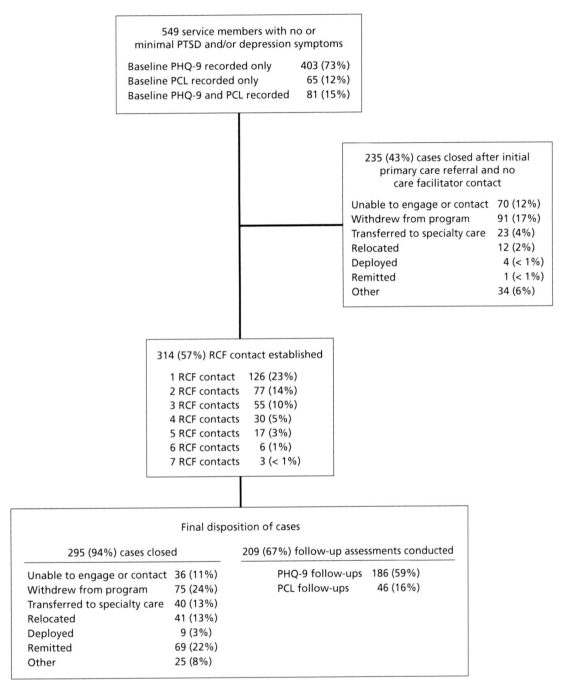

549 service members with no or
minimal PTSD and/or depression symptoms

Baseline PHQ-9 recorded only	403 (73%)
Baseline PCL recorded only	65 (12%)
Baseline PHQ-9 and PCL recorded	81 (15%)

235 (43%) cases closed after initial
primary care referral and no
care facilitator contact

Unable to engage or contact	70 (12%)
Withdrew from program	91 (17%)
Transferred to specialty care	23 (4%)
Relocated	12 (2%)
Deployed	4 (< 1%)
Remitted	1 (< 1%)
Other	34 (6%)

314 (57%) RCF contact established

1 RCF contact	126 (23%)
2 RCF contacts	77 (14%)
3 RCF contacts	55 (10%)
4 RCF contacts	30 (5%)
5 RCF contacts	17 (3%)
6 RCF contacts	6 (1%)
7 RCF contacts	3 (< 1%)

Final disposition of cases

295 (94%) cases closed

Unable to engage or contact	36 (11%)
Withdrew from program	75 (24%)
Transferred to specialty care	40 (13%)
Relocated	41 (13%)
Deployed	9 (3%)
Remitted	69 (22%)
Other	25 (8%)

209 (67%) follow-up assessments conducted

PHQ-9 follow-ups	186 (59%)
PCL follow-ups	46 (16%)

RAND *RR588-3.8*

CHAPTER FOUR

Facilitators and Barriers to RESPECT-Mil Implementation: Findings from Provider Discussions

While examining factors associated with the maintenance or sustainability of the RESPECT-Mil program, we conducted discussions with RESPECT-Mil providers (i.e., RCFs, BHCs, PCCs, and PCPs) to understand the facilitators and barriers to program implementation. Discussions were facilitated by a RAND Ph.D.-level researcher while another research team member recorded notes. The discussion facilitator checked and validated the notes and reconciled with the note taker any discrepancies or additions. Quotes from the discussions were then pile sorted into key themes. We developed an outline of the findings that would cover the basic themes that emerged. Within each section, we reexamined the quotes for a particular theme across provider types, taking into account the source of the quote (e.g., site), degree of adherence to the RESPECT-Mil program, and placement within the discussion in order to properly understand the quote in context. For each theme, we summarized the main ideas, identified benefits and challenges, and noted the variability in opinions. (More-detailed descriptions of the methods and analytic approach are provided in Chapter Three and Appendix L.)

Results of the provider discussions are presented in the subsequent sections. The first section describes participants' overall impressions of RESPECT-Mil. The next three sections of the results are organized according to the 3CM of integrating behavioral health treatment into primary care, as described in Chapter One.

The first component, PCPs and prepared practice, contains analyses of the themes most relevant to this component:

- the PCC's role
- decisionmaking: primary care versus behavioral health
- screening and facilitating treatment access
- prescribing and managing medication
- staffing, training, and turnover.

The next section corresponds to the second component, the RCF. The themes we discuss in this section are:

- the RCF's role
- RCF coordination and collaboration with other providers
- tracking and documenting service member information
- treatment: adherence, nonresponse, and side effects.

The third component of the 3CM is the BHC, which is the topic of the fourth section. The fifth section of this chapter describes our analysis of discussion content relevant to the quality monitoring of the implementation of RESPECT-Mil. These sections do not include multiple themes.

Finally, we end with a discussion of participants' responses related to addressing the behavioral health concerns of service members in general.

Overall Impressions of the RESPECT-Mil Program

At the outset of the discussions, we asked providers for their overall impression of the RESPECT-Mil program. Many of the respondents (17 of 35) had favorable impressions of the program, calling it "effective," "useful," and "rewarding" and saying that it "helps service members." About the same number (16 of 35) expressed more mixed impressions, citing similar strengths of the program but simultaneously pointing out challenges around screening, service member uptake, implementation and staffing, and tracking down service members. Only two respondents expressed predominantly negative opinions of the program, citing it as being difficult from a provider perspective or citing multiple issues with data systems, staffing, and roles.

There appeared to be some difference in overall impressions across the different types of providers. BHCs were predominantly positive in their opinions, with five of seven expressing positive opinions about the program (two were mixed, and zero were negative). RCFs were also positive about the program, with 7 of the 13 participating RCFs expressing predominantly positive impressions (five were mixed, and one was negative). PCCs and PCPs predominantly expressed more mixed opinions: PCCs could be classified as mixed in five of eight discussions (two were positive, and one was negative), and PCPs could be classified as mixed in four of seven discussions (three were positive, and zero were negative).

Primary Care Providers and Prepared Practice

Primary Care Champion Role

The main function of the PCC is to oversee the PCPs at their clinics, supporting them in their role and acting as a liaison with the RMIT. In this section we describe respondents' impressions of the PCCs, including the benefits of the PCC role as well as the challenges and limitations related to serving in this role.

General Impressions

Most respondents indicated that the PCC serves as a liaison between RCFs and PCPs and is responsible for training, supervising, and monitoring the PCPs in their implementation of RESPECT-Mil. For example, one PCC said, "The care facilitator and administrative assistant see all the MEDCOM Form 774 forms, PHQ, PCL, and I'll get the [list of patients who need follow-up]. They've identified issues with patients but no one is following up or something may have been done but it's not being documented. When they tell me there is a problem, I go around and talk to the specific providers." An RCF added, "The PCC is in charge of any issues with the PCPs. If there are issues with referrals or paperwork, then the PCC approaches PCPs."

One RCF spoke about how helpful the PCC can be in this role, as well as in monitoring PCPs: "Communication with the medical champion and providers is good. The medical champion has been very involved and calls daily to see if we are doing OK. She's involved in the administrative part of what we do. She is very supportive and responsive to problems with providers."

There was one respondent who did not refer to these tasks as part of the PCC role. This PCC said that the role mainly involved administrative tasks: "I answered emails, approved timecards, and dealt with the union. Nothing I did as PCC was medically related."

Benefits

This liaison function was widely seen as the main benefit of the PCC role, particularly in aiding communication between the RCF and PCPs.

Challenges and Limitations

Respondents referred to two main challenges to playing the PCC role effectively: (1) time and resource constraints and (2) the resistance of PCPs and RCFs.

Time and Resource Constraints

Many respondents suggested that both PCCs and PCPs felt as though there was insufficient time and resources—including staff and physical space—to implement RESPECT-Mil effectively. One PCC said, "The bottom line is time. It takes more time to discuss [mental health] with the patient, and the PCP has limited time in their visit to discuss these issues." A PCP explained, "I think RESPECT-Mil can be useful, but there is just a lot going on at this site right now."

To address this challenge, some respondents suggested allocating a greater portion of the PCC's time to RESPECT-Mil. Others recommended hiring more staff and providing more physical space so that PCPs can more easily meet with patients to discuss behavioral health.

PCP and RCF Resistance

Some respondents noted that, in addition to time and resource constraints, some PCPs "haven't bought in" to RESPECT-Mil. A PCC noted that while most PCPs do implement the program, some "don't do the program because it takes extra time and there is a desire to not handle anything related to mental health." The lack of comfort with behavioral health–related issues experienced by some providers was also mentioned by an RCF, who said: "I don't believe the providers have even looked at their manual. They have a lot going on and I think a lot don't feel comfortable with behavioral health." One PCC also reported that the RCF was not effectively implementing RESPECT-Mil: "I have RCFs with high caseloads who aren't doing anything." This type of resistance may interfere with the implementation of the program, although only a few respondents mentioned it.

Decisionmaking: Primary Care Versus Behavioral Health

When a patient presents to a primary care clinic with behavioral health problems, the provider must decide whether the patient's behavioral health condition can be treated within primary care (i.e., within RESPECT-Mil), or if he or she should be referred for specialty care, as in a behavioral health clinic. In this section we discuss respondents' views on this issue and how they described making such decisions.

General Impressions

Many respondents discussed the criteria used to decide whether to refer a symptomatic service member to RESPECT-Mil, continue treatment within the primary care setting, or refer the service member to behavioral health. While some providers said that they always refer service members to behavioral health or always to RESPECT-Mil, the majority reported that symptom severity and complexity determined where to refer service members. Most providers (including BHCs, PCCs, RCFs, and PCPs) indicated that they generally refer service members to RESPECT-Mil, but when symptoms are severe, complex, or require more-intensive services, they refer to behavioral health. For example, a PCC said, "When we are talking dual medications for dual disorders, I'll sit down with the patient and tell them that we are crossing over into behavioral health territory."

Some respondents noted that they consider existing services and aim to avoid duplication of effort; if a service member is already receiving treatment from a psychiatrist in behavioral health, they will not refer to RESPECT-Mil. Providers also highlighted service member preferences as important to the referral process: "If they screen positive, we use the PHQ or PCL, and then we talk to them and see if they need a referral to mental health or RESPECT-Mil and determine with the patient what's best for them."

Respondents identified two major factors that could influence decisions about whether to refer to behavioral health or RESPECT-Mil. These were (1) their views about the value of primary care–based treatment and (2) PCPs' comfort treating mental health problems.

Value of Primary Care–Based Mental Health Treatment

Several respondents thought that primary care–based services could help reach a broader population that otherwise would not have received mental health care, either because of long wait lists in behavioral health or because patients' symptoms would not have come to light. According to one RCF, "[RESPECT-Mil] has given patients and providers better resources. Some patients would have fallen through the cracks because they aren't symptomatic enough to warrant a behavioral health referral or refused behavioral health, but this allows them to engage with the PCP to get resources." Some respondents also said that they thought the treatment provided by RESPECT-Mil was effective for the vast majority of service members with mild to moderate depression and PTSD, and that the program frees up time for behavioral health providers to devote more resources to service members with more complex and severe problems. A BHC stated, "In behavioral health we are understaffed and scrambling to serve patients. This program makes it more manageable. By taking the cases that can be treated in primary care and those who are not inclined to seek behavioral health, it gives us the opportunity in behavioral health to focus on the more severe cases."

PCP Comfort Treating Mental Health Problems

Many respondents said that despite the potential value of primary care–based mental health services like RESPECT-Mil, whether service members are referred to the program depends on the comfort level of the PCPs who are managing treatment. Some PCPs said that they felt extremely comfortable treating mental health disorders, but many respondents emphasized that PCPs' discomfort assessing and treating mental health problems has been a challenge. For example, a BHC said that RESPECT-Mil "doesn't work when PCPs are uncomfortable with behavioral health. We see that they don't want to prescribe meds, or talk to patients about behavioral health issues." A few PCPs said that they feel particularly uncomfortable diagnosing and treating PTSD: "I feel PTSD needs a longer appointment and I feel it goes beyond primary care."

Some respondents suggested that PCP discomfort could be related to fears about the risks involved in treating service members with mental health problems, as well as about the time and effort involved. One BHC said, "There is not a lot that incentivizes a PCP to keep a service member with a behavioral health issue because they take so much time and there are risks with those service members' care. PCPs think it would be easy to make a behavioral health service member not their problem. They can just click a button and the person is referred to behavioral health." A PCC agreed that some PCPs "don't do the program because it takes extra time and there is a desire to not handle anything related to mental health."

Screening and Facilitating Treatment Access

One of the key objectives of RESPECT-Mil is to improve the screening of depression and PTSD in primary care and to help those who screen positively to access treatment. In this section we discuss respondents' views on how this process works, its benefits, and challenges and limitations to screening and facilitating treatment access.

General Impressions

Respondents' descriptions of the process of screening and facilitating treatment access were generally aligned with the RESPECT-Mil treatment manual guidelines. The majority of respondents also indicated that the screening process was going smoothly.

Benefits

Many respondents spoke about the screening of service members in primary care as an important and valuable aspect of the program, because it "gets patients on the radar screen" who are at risk for PTSD or depression and those with suicidal ideation, who would otherwise "fall through the cracks." Consistent and structured screening opens the door for service members and providers to recognize, acknowledge, and dialogue about mental health issues in a less threatening and stigmatizing environment. (As one respondent commented, "Service members see it as having less stigma than behavioral health.")

Challenges and Limitations

Respondents also noted several challenges. Some PCCs and RCFs mentioned that some PCPs refused to use the screening forms or refer service members to RESPECT-Mil. Most PCPs who we spoke with also mentioned time constraints. One said, "I need more than the allotted 15-minute appointment time. The appointments are more like 30 minutes when a patient has PTSD and or depression." Providers also expressed concerns about false negative screens (i.e., service members who are not forthright about their symptoms), the inefficiency of screening service members who are already in RESPECT-Mil or in behavioral health, screening fatigue given other touch points (e.g., the Post Deployment Health Reassessment), the inability to account for behavioral issues that are due to situational factors, and more-severe cases (e.g., psychosis, bipolar disorder).

Some PCCs and RCFs talked about ways they had overcome these barriers to improve adherence to the screening protocol, such as a discussion with PCPs about the rationale for the program and related screeners, thanking PCPs when they used data from the screening tools to facilitate treatment, and enlisting the support of command. Other PCCs relayed that there was no enforcement at the local level but referred to performance reports issued by RESPECT-Mil, while another PCC expressed a desire for a "carrot and stick" to enforce provider compliance after describing that "one provider hid the RESPECT-Mil screening forms."

Prescribing and Managing Medication

Prescribing and managing medications for depression and PTSD is a key function of PCPs in the RESPECT-Mil program. In this section we discuss respondents' general impressions of how this works within RESPECT-Mil as well as the challenges that providers experience in prescribing and managing behavioral health medications in a primary care setting.

General Impressions

Many respondents noted that RESPECT-Mil has helped to provide the level of careful monitoring and attention that is needed to properly prescribe and manage medications for depression and PTSD. As one PCC noted, "[RESPECT-Mil] provides really good follow-up for those on medications. Patients can talk to someone and maybe prevent them from stopping taking their medications."

Challenges

PCCs and PCPs indicated varying levels of comfort prescribing and managing psychotropic medications. Some PCCs and PCPs reported feeling uncomfortable prescribing any medications to treat behavioral health problems ("I'm not comfortable with prescribing medications"), while others felt comfortable prescribing only for noncomplex cases ("If the behavioral health issue is straightforward, then initiating medical therapy is usually what I end up doing. If there is a complicated case, as it usually is, the patient may need a polypharm consultation"). According to some RCFs and PCCs, PCPs do consult with RCFs and BHCs when treating service members with more-complex behavioral health problems or those experiencing side effects.

Staffing, Training, and Turnover

High-quality implementation of any program requires attention to the way staff are selected and trained, as well as to how staff turnover is handled. We asked respondents about how these issues are addressed within RESPECT-Mil at their clinics. We describe their responses below.

PCC and PCP Staffing and Training

With respect to training, we heard diametrically opposed views from two PCCs. One reported receiving no formal training and had to learn on the job and in the monthly calls with the RMIT. The other reported receiving training and that it was helpful, but that since the training, there had not been enough guidance or support. Both of these PCCs said the position takes up a lot more time than they expected.

Although many respondents indicated that it was the PCC's responsibility to train PCPs (see the PCC role section), some said that RCFs had taken on this task. Of the respondents who discussed PCP training, most said that despite attempts to conduct more-formalized group training sessions, they found this to be difficult due to PCP time constraints. Many reported that ad hoc training and refreshers occurred via email, telephone, or individual face-to-face meetings. PCP views on RESPECT-Mil training varied, with some lamenting a lack of training ("there was no real orientation to the program") and others praising the training quality ("the training was good").

Turnover

Respondents revealed a range of views on how staff turnover affects implementation. Some said that turnover had minimal impact at their sites ("staff turnover has not been an issue yet"), but most agreed that "staff turnover is a problem." Respondents stressed the importance of training new staff immediately in order to minimize confusion and disruptions to service provision. Some recommended hiring civilian employees as often as possible, because they are less likely to move frequently and thus could provide more stability.

Care Facilitators

RESPECT-Mil Care Facilitator Roles

The role of the RCF is to support the service member through the course of treatment and to support the PCP by promoting service member adherence to the treatment plan. The RCF provides service members with psychoeducation, supports their treatment preferences, and monitors adherence and response to treatment. As a liaison between the service member and the PCP, the RCF communicates the service member's experience to the PCP and ensures that the service member's needs are addressed. In this section, we describe respondents' impressions of the role of the RCF, the benefits of having an RCF, and the challenges that espondents noted in serving as or working with RCFs.

General Impressions

Descriptions of RCF activities typically reflected many of the roles and responsibilities outlined by RESPECT-Mil (see Chapter One). A number of RCFs spoke of being aligned with the RESPECT-Mil program. One stated, "I follow the manual." Another said, "We make sure we align ourselves with our protocol." Several RCFs asserted going "above and beyond" and doing "more than what is in the manual." For example, one RCF reported, "Providers put in consults not for RESPECT-Mil, but the consult request will say please assist with coordinating care to behavioral health. . . . I almost have another caseload of people that aren't enrolled. . . . I don't get compensated in any way on relative value units or workload credit." In contrast, another RCF stated, "I am not familiar with the RESPECT-Mil manual. I have worked out my own system for implementation. My system is the way that care should be delivered." In addition, some providers shared negative impressions of RCF performance. For example, one PCC stated, "I have RCFs with high caseloads who aren't doing anything. . . . All the RCFs are doing is killing our numbers."

Benefits

According to BHCs, RCFs "provide a means of leveraging our different roles" by serving as a "point person for care" and providing information on the "rhythm of the clinic." PCCs described RCFs performing as a safety function by checking on forms, alerting providers of the "more serious" service members who "aren't caught by providers," and providing "monthly notes" on "how the patient is doing." One PCC highlighted the value of RCFs to service members, stating: "Patients have come to rely on them. They've been a good friend to them when care is limited." One PCP also expressed similar benefits, noting: "The RCF takes the stress off in contacting patients, scrubs the medical charts, and coordinates care."

Challenges and Limitations

Respondents noted several challenges associated with the RCF role. For example, respondents noted problems with some RCFs that included failure to contact service members within seven to ten days of the initial referral, the provision of untimely and poor quality feedback, and not making the four-week follow-up calls. According to one PCC, "Often it took six months for the follow-up, and at that point it was too late." Another PCC acknowledged that "there are many nurses who are inconsistent with phone calls, . . . but sometimes it is hard to contact patients even if they make several calls." One RCF shared more-extreme examples of problematic performance: "Some of these RCFs have only seen one patient in three months." Another said, "One person told me about a site where they never come to work and they are writing notes about what they did. I think this happens more so than not." One PCC noted that it was difficult to determine RCF contact rate because the system does not aggregate numbers by personnel, while another PCC expressed that it "would help for RCFs to know what other RCFs are doing," referring to an RCF who did 180 snapshots a month, which may put RCFs "performance in perspective."

Respondents also noted problems with RCFs' inappropriate or ineffective use of time. One RCF noted, "As a care facilitator . . . you are not authorized or qualified to counsel anybody. . . . I have observed people in RESPECT-Mil stepping outside of their role to provide counseling." One PCC stated, "I point out that they don't need to spend four hours to prepare for a call. . . . The calls should only be 20 minutes and not longer. . . . They aren't therapists." However, several RCFs asserted that they knew their roles were not to be counselors. One RCF stated, "I am not the person to pour your heart out to—if I said the wrong thing, I would make it worse."

RCF Coordination and Collaboration with Other Providers

RCFs are expected to help coordinate patient care and collaborate with other providers, such as the PCPs and BHC at his or her site. This section details respondents' views on how this process is going at their clinics, including what is going well and what they believe interferes with effective coordination and collaboration between the RCF and other providers.

General Impressions

Most respondents reported that they thought coordination of care and collaboration among staff was going quite well in the program. Means of communication among providers was varied, and included electronic data systems (AHLTA), notes via the T-Cons module, email, telephone, and face-to-face methods. For many, face-to-face contacts were preferred ("one thing we have done recently to improve coordination and monitoring is to put RCFs into the clinics"), but others valued having everything well documented in the AHLTA record. Though respondents often described relying on AHLTA and T-Cons to update providers about service member treatment planning, some exceptions were noted. One BHC relayed the process of interacting with RCFs face-to-face initially and then conducting staffing through AHLTA only "after learning the skills and capacity" of RCFs. In addition, one PCP noted, "I will walk the patient down to RESPECT-Mil" if more attention is needed, but will otherwise send the "paperwork and referral through the computer."

Benefits

Solid linkages between PCPs and the RCFs were highlighted by several respondents, with one PCP noting: "It's like having an extra arm." In terms of patient care, this coordination was seen as helpful for the patient. For example, one RCF said, "The patients will tell the PCP that they take medications, but then the same service members will tell me that they don't take their medications and then I will alert the PCP to change their medication to find a good fit."

Challenges and Limitations

Respondents noted several coordination challenges. One of these was that the RCFs were not automatically notified of whether PCPs follow BHC recommendations. One RCF explained: "Providers acknowledge communication in AHLTA but did not address any of the issues in the visit with the patient." A few RCFs described needing to check the AHLTA records to see if any changes were made to medications or if the service member was called back in, rather than hearing directly from the provider.

A few respondents noted that they "felt unsure" about their referrals to behavioral health, did not know the providers there well, or did not know whether service members they referred had followed through and gotten care. Similarly, a few respondents said that having better access to behavioral health, particularly on-site in the primary care clinic, would enhance the program. One RCF stated, "I am the link to behavioral health, but I feel like it could be better."

One communication challenge noted by a few respondents was the need to document the same materials in multiple places or to document more than one communication. As one RCF reported, "Documentation for these visits is very lengthy, in narrative summary form. I have to document both in AHLTA and also in FIRST-STEPS. The same exact information goes in both."

Finally, two PCPs expressed frustration with the RESPECT-Mil program. One noted never having interacted with any RCFs or BHCs, and another reported rarely making referrals into the program because feedback was that the service members who were referred needed specialty care and were "out of scope" for RESPECT-Mil.

Tracking and Documenting Service Member Information

We asked respondents about how they track and document information about service members' symptoms and treatment progress. In this section we summarize respondents' views about the benefits and challenges of tracking and documenting such information.

General Impressions

Respondents reported documenting and sending service member information to other providers using a variety of methods, including communicating via phone, in person, email, video teleconferencing, and T-Cons sent through AHLTA. Respondents also talked about the benefits and challenges associated with using FIRST-STEPS.

Benefits

One PCC commented on the benefit of "solid documentation within patients' charts," given that "communication happens all through emails and AHLTA notes." Another PCC noted that the MEDCOM Form 774 "actually helps" and makes the PCP's note better, but acknowledged that "some people treat it as a burden."

Several RCFs commented positively about FIRST-STEPS, describing it as "fairly easy to navigate" and "an amazing program" that "takes you from start to finish." RCFs talked about the usefulness of "the tickler function," which inputs all the appointments, allowing RCFs to see which patients are due for follow-ups. One RCF also noted that there are constant efforts "to improve the system to make it user-friendly" and "effective for the service members."

Some BHCs also related positive experiences interacting with FIRST-STEPS. One BHC stated, "FIRST-STEPS is a good tool. I like the visual component. . . . It shows if a patient is getting better or worse."

Challenges and Limitations

RCFs also reported some technical concerns with FIRST-STEPS. One relayed that one of the screens had been changed without any review, making it "the only part that isn't useful." RCFs also noted some technical issues with FIRST-STEPS ("if you don't save, it erases what you put in" and "every now and then it goes down").

RCFs also discussed problems associated with FIRST-STEPS not being connected to AHLTA. RCFs conveyed that they "do a lot of duplication of work that takes a lot of time." As described by one PCC, "The nurses do double work by putting information in FIRST-STEPS and then putting a T-Cons in AHLTA." Another RCF asserted that FIRST-STEPS "should be on a local level, just like AHLTA" so that people can "log in," "see what's going on," and hold providers accountable, "but right now there is no accountability in FIRST-STEPS."

Some BHCs expressed uncertainty as to whether BHCs could access FIRST-STEPS or they referred to FIRST-STEPS as a tool mainly for RCFs. Another BHC noted, "With the roll-out of the behavioral health data platform, FIRST-STEPS isn't really helpful. The RCFs find it helpful. I find it cumbersome as one of seven databases that I have to monitor. The system itself is good, but I wish it talked to others."

Several PCCs and PCPs pointed out the difficulties associated with the lack of integration between AHLTA and FIRST-STEPS. One PCC noted that "RESPECT-Mil does not work with AHLTA, so it is difficult to coordinate across systems." Another PCC stated, "It is a problem that FIRST-STEPS is disconnected from AHLTA" and remarked that the data are "not accurate" because FIRST-STEPS will miss service member care contacts recorded via AHLTA but not RESPECT-Mil.

Treatment: Adherence, Nonresponse, and Side Effects

We also asked providers about how treatment adherence, nonresponse, and side effects are handled within RESPECT-Mil at their sites. In what follows, we describe respondents' views on how these issues are addressed and the challenges they have encountered.

General Impressions

Respondents referred to relying on RCFs to track service members' progress. However, there were different perspectives about who is responsible for supporting service member treatment adherence. One BHC asserted that it "is the PCP's job to ensure compliance," whereas one PCC stated: "It's a BHC issue." Another PCC noted, "The PCP is supposed to correct nonadherence if the RCF cannot do it. The RCF is the first line of defense, then the issue goes to the BHC or PCP." RCFs often reported staffing nonadherent service members with BHCs and sending a T-Con to notify the PCPs. RCFs spoke about the various challenges encountered with addressing service member treatment nonadherence, nonresponse, and medication side effects and the different strategies they employed.

Challenges of Contacting Service Members

In order to monitor and ensure treatment adherence, RCFs must periodically follow up with service members. Many RCFs spoke about the challenges involved with not being able to reach service members by phone. RCFs described difficulties such as spending "a lot of time trying to get in touch with someone just to find out that they want to disenroll from the program," staying in contact with "patients who have changed their number," and it being "hard to catch" the "many people coming and going" due to deployment, permanent change of station, or block leave. RCFs reported a variety of strategies to reach service members, including calling, emailing, and leaving voicemails; doing "investigative work in AHLTA to track them down"; asking service members to "stop by or before or after other appointments on site"; and scheduling more flexibly (e.g., calling and setting up a time to talk the week that a call is due). One RCF discussed going to service members' chains of command but opined, "ultimately the service members wouldn't have to attend the appointment" because RESPECT-Mil is "voluntary and confidential."

A number of RCFs talked about the importance of having face-to-face contact with service members, particularly during the initial visit. RCFs noted that "without the initial face-to-face engagement, it is more difficult to bring the service members in" and that "patients come in because they like face-to-face contact." One RCF remarked that "patients are more relaxed in person. . . . On the phone they are at work, busy, in a hurry, etc." Another RCF talked about not having "the benefit of watching body language or affect" over the phone and in one instance being "able to pull psychosis out of a patient" during an in-person visit by seeing that the service member was responding to internal stimuli. One RCF also described administering the 17-item PCL "word for word" over the phone as "ridiculous."

Medication Side Effects, Nonresponse, and Nonadherence

In addition to consulting with providers, RCFs reported providing service members with education and guidance on how to deal with medication side effects (e.g., suggesting new times for taking medication, inviting patients in to discuss another medication). One RCF reported tracking service members who do not want medications to see if they feel more depressed after a few months, or to encourage them to stay on medications, but that many times service members will not answer their phone calls. For service members who are not responding to or improving on medications, one RCF relayed that "the BHC and PCC try to figure it out." However, another RCF reported: "The manual gives them three months, but I give them two months before referral to behavioral health." One RCF noted, "Many times patients cannot or don't want to engage in counseling. . . . My goal is to get the service members to overcome whatever is holding them back from getting care. . . . If service members don't want to go, I can't force them." RCFs noted a variety of reasons for treatment nonadherence, such as: patients "quit because the counselor is an idiot," service members are "so driven for their career . . . [that] they can't function on their medications so they miss them," and the "command" or "unit won't let them off for counseling." One RCF relayed working with service members to get another counselor if their current counselor was not working out, and another RCF shared that the officer in charge was able to work out problems with the unit, allowing time off for appointments.

Behavioral Health Champions

The BHC is a psychiatrist who serves as a component of the service member's care team. The BHC provides clinical and pharmacotherapy advice to the PCP, discusses the service member's progress with the RCF, and facilitates referrals to specialty care when indicated or requested. In this section, we describe respondents' views on the role of the BHC, the benefits of having a BHC, and the challenges and limitations associated with the BHC role.

General Impressions

Respondents described the BHC role in a way that was generally in line with the RESPECT-Mil model (see Chapter One). They described the BHC role as one of "mentor" or "coach" to the PCPs, with activities ranging from making specific recommendations for specific service members, to more general teaching about psychotropic medications, suicide assessment, or other topics related to PTSD and depression. A few BHCs described having a role in educating PCPs as they turned over, which is as a way to orient them to behavioral health generally in order to prepare them for RESPECT-Mil.

Benefits

In general, there was a sense that the process of "staffing" cases, or meeting with the BHC to discuss the RCF's caseload, was beneficial. As one respondent described it,

> I review each case at the beginning, in the middle (if the patient isn't getting better), and at the end, before they leave the program. If the patient is not improving, I suggest increasing the dose or switching medications. In terms of side effects, sometimes the RCF brings those to my attention, and I suggest a change in medication to the PCP.

Challenges and Limitations

However, most BHCs and at least one RCF mentioned that there was not enough time to devote to RESPECT-Mil given their other duties in behavioral health, and that high caseloads made it difficult to spend as much time on cases as desired. Several respondents explained that not having a BHC who was employed by RESPECT-Mil, and was instead pulled from other duties, was detrimental to the program, and a few suggested that having a full-time BHC would enhance the program. In particular, respondents from higher-volume sites said that they could only attend to new cases and cases that needed to be closed, rather than being able to review cases that were in the middle of treatment. For instance, one BHC said, in the process of explaining why additional time, or smaller caseloads, would be helpful: "I think the BHC should allot more time to go into FIRST-STEPS to monitor people they've made recommendations for, to do a sampling on how the program is working." One site described a creative solution to this problem, in which staff augmented the RESPECT-Mil budget with core funds to bolster the RESPECT-Mil BHC position, and found a way to document RESPECT-Mil productivity to "get credit" for consulting on RESPECT-Mil cases to justify the expenditure of funds.

In addition, some mentioned the challenge in working with the minority of PCPs who were not fully on board with the program. For instance, one BHC stated that about 10 percent of the time there was a reluctance to act on recommended changes in medication: "The PCPs are . . . overwhelmed by their patient panel, . . . but sometimes it seemed that there was resistance to receiving the recommendation."

There was variability in responses regarding training for the BHC position, with some saying the training provided was helpful and others saying it was not. One respondent criticized the program for not having clearer "standard operating procedures" such that each site could set up the program within general guidelines, rather than having the program fully delineated.

Quality Monitoring

We asked providers to tell us about how the quality of aspects of the RESPECT-Mil program is monitored. In this section, we detail respondents' views on how program quality is monitored, including what is working well and what needs to be improved.

General Impressions

When asked about how different components of the RESPECT-Mil program are monitored for quality, many respondents said that there is "very little" or no monitoring, though some described informal methods of peer-to-peer supervision or quality monitoring, and most acknowledged getting reports from the RMIT on a periodic basis and participating in monthly site calls with the RMIT. Overall, there was a good deal of variability in opinions on this aspect of the program, which varied to some degree by role.

Benefits

Three aspects of the program were identified by respondents as being a means to monitor quality: the role of the RCF, who monitors service members and thus has direct information about the performance of the PCPs; the FIRST-STEPS system, which helps RCFs structure their monitoring of service members over time; and the periodic feedback of metrics to sites by the RMIT. Although these aspects were described by many respondents, there was some criticism of each. On the other hand, feedback from respondents on the monthly site calls with the RMIT was much more mixed, with only about half seeing benefits, such as being "helpful" or "useful" as a place where one is able to "ask stupid questions and fine-tune." A few respondents mentioned that site visits were helpful in identifying problems and developing a plan for resolving them.

In addition, several respondents talked about informal methods of quality monitoring, such as peer-to-peer feedback and peer review of AHLTA notes. As one RCF noted, "We monitor each other constantly to provide the best care to the service member."

Challenges and Limitations

RCFs described getting only limited feedback from their direct supervisor (the PCC). "My PCC is not involved," noted one respondent. "Some feedback would be good," said another. Despite several comments about FIRST-STEPS being useful in helping them monitor service members, quality monitoring through FIRST-STEPS and monthly reports from the RMIT were also seen as problematic by some RCFs. A few noted that FIRST-STEPS does not document all their efforts in outreach to service members, that the reports describe the past rather than the present, and that it is possible to falsify entries in FIRST-STEPS. In addition, the metrics report data at the clinic level, so FIRST-STEPS does not provide feedback to individuals about their performances. Most respondents saw very little in the way of monitoring the coordination of care within RESPECT-Mil, with much more focus on screening rates and contact with service members.

Monthly site calls with the RMIT were criticized by several respondents as being a "waste of time" and more about numbers than problem solving. As one respondent said, "If they provided tools for improvement, the calls would be better." There was also some criticism of the RMIT being in Washington, D.C., rather than local, and that the RMIT did not understand the local issues that made a site different.

BHCs described very little monitoring, except for peer-to-peer monitoring through behavioral health. One respondent suggested that the metrics on RESPECT-Mil were "cruddy" but that it would be helpful to get feedback from service members, RCFs, and PCPs on his or her performance.

Despite some discussion of peer review and quality, other respondents made such comments as: "It's pretty autonomous as far as the calling and screening," and "I am basically implementing it to the best of my ability. . . . I am the only one that is here. There is no peer review of that process."

Addressing the Behavioral Health Concerns of Service Members

The RESPECT-Mil program has changed the way the military health system addresses service members' behavioral health needs. We asked respondents to comment on what needs to change the most now in the way that the military health system addresses the behavioral health concerns of service members. Respondents commented on several issues, highlighting:

- stigma around mental health problems and treatment seeking
- capacity issues in the provision of behavioral health
- the need to engage command more around behavioral health issues
- the disability system
- the needs of service members' support systems and families
- the comparison of RESPECT-Mil with other initiatives like PCMH.

Several respondents discussed the stigma around mental health services, and some of them talked about the way in which the RESPECT-Mil program has already helped to reduce stigma. One RCF noted, "[RESPECT-Mil] helped service members out tremendously with stigma. PTSD was coming to the forefront at that time. Since then, we have helped a number of service members. . . . Now there is less and less stigma." However, other respondents pointed out that both negative perceptions about mental health and treatment and service members' perceptions that treatment might harm their careers or ability to maintain a security clearance were deterrents to getting mental health care, and this was a central issue in improving mental health.

Respondents also talked about the need for better access to specialty mental health care, the need for more providers, and the benefits of embedding behavioral health assets into the primary care setting. One asserted that "service members are still not able to access behavioral health care," and noted that the waiting list at his or her behavioral health clinic was about three months.

Several respondents talked about the need to engage command more in addressing behavioral health issues, from suggestions about education to the need for routine screening at the unit level, to being more open to mental health care. In particular, a few respondents said that commanders did not always allow or support mental health or other medical appointments, and they sometimes had the attitude that service members should "buck up" and handle mental health problems on their own. Others suggested that behavioral health assets be embedded into the brigade. One PCC proposed, "The biggest thing they need to do is to get the assets out to where the patients are. . . . Embed behavioral assets into the brigade." A few also suggested that the ways that command treats service members are part of the problem: "[They are] mistreated or not taken seriously by their command."

A few respondents also noted problems with the disability and compensation system within the military, and that it rewards failure rather than success. One respondent commented, "The disability compensation system rewards not getting better. We should incentivize recovery."

A few respondents also commented on the need to attend to service members' support systems or families. One respondent noted, "We ask a lot about the individual but not about their support systems and if they make life better or worse. . . . For some service members, it might be better to have their support system come in with them to talk."

We also asked respondents to comment on how RESPECT-Mil is similar to or different from other behavioral health initiatives, such as the PCMH model. Here there was also variability, with some respondents seeing the possibility that the two initiatives could be compatible and others expressing concern about how they might compete with one another. A few different respondents noted that having an embedded mental health specialist within primary care (part of the PCMH model) would help to enhance RESPECT-Mil, but that perhaps the mental health specialist needed to be able to provide longer-term treatment than in the PCMH model. Others expressed concerns about "too many initiatives" and programs "competing for the same resources." As one respondent put it, "There are too many orders out there with too many people saying different things. Put out one order that supersedes all of the smaller orders and put together a comprehensive behavioral package."

CHAPTER FIVE

Facilitators and Barriers to RESPECT-Mil Implementation: Findings from RMIT Discussions

In this chapter, we present the results stemming from discussions with staff from the RMIT, who provided their perspectives on facilitators and barriers to implementing the RESPECT-Mil program. The 11-member implementation team is composed of directors, behavioral health proponents, RCF proponents, program evaluators, database managers and analysts, and administrative assistants. The implementation team had the responsibility of providing training, program management, oversight and monitoring, and technical assistance to RESPECT-Mil sites. We begin with a summary of general impressions of the implementation process, as well as of internal RMIT processes and functioning.

Next we present findings from questions about specific implementation components. RMIT members were asked to comment on their roles and responsibilities with respect to program implementation at the site level—specifically, their involvement in the following:

- preparing the practice
- hiring, staffing, and turnover
- training and support
- RMIT monitoring, including performance reports, monthly site calls, and site visits
- incentives.

Finally, we explore bigger-picture questions about the influences of the larger Army health care system on the RMIT, issues identified by the RMIT team surrounding mental health care in the Army, and the transition to the PCMH model.

Overall Impressions

Overall, RMIT respondents viewed their roles and responsibilities as having a positive impact on the implementation of RESPECT-Mil and on improving behavioral health care for service members. Respondents perceived that they had the most impact in the following areas: "perpetuating the concept" of integrated treatment; the development of the FIRST-STEPS data monitoring system; the monitoring and support provided to sites through calls, visits, screening tools, and performance reports; and efforts to help reduce suicide among service members.

RMIT Internal Processes and Functioning

Individuals from the RMIT team were asked to comment on how the RMIT functions and to note its strengths and challenges. Most said that the RMIT staff work hard, are busy, and enjoy working together. Some also thought that "having clearly defined and distinct roles" and having "representatives from different specialties and disciplines" made the team more effective.

RMIT respondents expressed a range of views about how well the RMIT communicates and executes its tasks. Some explained that "communication within RMIT works pretty well," while others communicated that "RMIT processes could be more efficient if they could be more autonomous and not wait for everything to be approved."

Many RMIT respondents also maintained that more staff were needed in order to effectively perform RMIT duties: "The size of RMIT inhibits us from doing a good job. We are too small, and we are stretched too thin."

In addition, some recommended improved monitoring of the RMIT: "There should be formal systems in place to evaluate what we are doing" in order to understand "what we are doing well and not doing well."

Preparing the Practice for RESPECT-Mil

A key role for RMIT team members is preparing the practice settings for implementation. During the site preparation training workshop, the RMIT provides an overview of the general RESPECT-Mil model and facilitates a discussion of factors to consider when planning for implementation. In collaboration with an RMIT staff member who is experienced and knowledgeable about the program model, the local RESPECT-Mil team develops an implementation plan that takes into consideration the characteristics and processes of the individual clinic. Then RCFs, BHCs, PCCs, and administrative assistants are trained to implement RESPECT-Mil. Continued training occurs "over time in coaching calls."

Respondents noted the importance of "getting the command element on board." For example, MEDCOM, Installation Command, the chief of primary care, and the chief of family medicine "have to buy in, assign a BHC and a PCC, and we need to train them." A respondent said that this "helps [RMIT] develop an implementation plan that is good for their site. Then they flesh it out and fine-tune it."

Respondents also discussed barriers to preparing the practice. Some talked about lack of motivation or reluctance among leadership and RESPECT-Mil staff, which can pose a challenge to implementation: "Those who resist the program, that are not familiar and don't like it, create the biggest problems for preparing the practice for RESPECT-Mil." Another RMIT member said that some "installations had issues because primary care leadership did not believe that behavioral health should be part of primary care. . . . Once those leaders rotated out, the program implementation at those sites went much better."

Some RMIT respondents also highlighted barriers related to a shortage of time and resources for RESPECT-Mil staff: "PCCs should be given some admin time so they can fulfill their tasks," and BHCs "have a lot of responsibilities and this is an additional one that they may not have even asked for."

Hiring, Staffing, and Turnover

Several RMIT respondents spoke about the hiring process for RESPECT-Mil positions. As one person described, "RMIT provides sites with position descriptions and confirms their funding, but the hiring is done on site, usually by nursing but sometimes by behavioral health or another department." Many indicated that the RMIT has little influence over who is assigned to positions such as BHC, PCC, and RCF. Some RMIT respondents stated that they would like to have more say in who is hired for these positions.

Some also said that "red tape" related to the hiring process can hinder program implementation: "It takes so long for positions to be posted, the interview process, the selection, and the review of applications. It can take several months and longer in Europe. It's just crippling to try to get a program going."

Consistent with comments from RESPECT-Mil providers, RMIT respondents talked about staff turnover as a challenge. They mentioned that the frequent moving of military personnel and their families can cause disruptions and long periods during which positions are unfilled, and therefore parts of the program may not be implemented effectively. In addition, "When a primary provider works consistently with a service member and they trust them and then they leave, it's a problem. Service members want to stay with the same primary care provider for the entire program." One individual said, "We recognized we should hire civilians who wouldn't be deploying any time soon." To address these issues, RMIT respondents said they "track vacant positions and start advocating to the installations to begin filling positions," but "RMIT is sometimes the last to know that people at the sites are leaving." According to another RMIT respondent, staff turnover is now a regular agenda item in the monthly site calls.

RMIT respondents also highlighted unfilled positions on their own team as a challenge: "Increasing the number of staff on the RMIT team in the proponent slots would help to cover the workload as the number of sites increases." Several RMIT respondents suggested allowing staff to work remotely in order to more efficiently fill open positions with well-qualified individuals.

Training and Support

Another responsibility of the RMIT is to provide training and support to RESPECT-Mil site staff. Respondents said that champion training used to be conducted in person, but it is now conducted online because the costs and time required for champions to travel to Washington, D.C., for in-person trainings were too high. One respondent said that the RMIT hopes to further develop multimodal trainings that can be conducted only online and through video teleconferencing, the telephone, and reading material.

RCFs are the only participants who continue to train in person in Washington, D.C., according to respondents. The training for RCFs lasts about three days, with approximately half a day spent on the FIRST-STEPS system. An RMIT staff member said, "That face-to-face training is very valuable because the nurses are the guts of the program, and if we can't maintain that connection with them, we'll see a lot of problems in fidelity."

Respondents recalled that when the PCCs were trained in person, they would spend part of the training developing an implementation plan, which they would bring back to their clinics. The PCCs are then responsible for training the PCPs, but "PCCs don't get admin time to do the RESPECT-Mil tasks, and that can be really hard."

A respondent added that RMIT staff now trains IBHCs "on what RESPECT-Mil is and how they can work with their on-site RESPECT-Mil team." IBHCs are psychologists and social workers who will be assigned to the primary care clinics under the PCMH model. However, one individual noted that "RMIT is short on trainers," and more are needed to fulfill the demand, because "RMIT is assisting with IBHC training across three services—the Army, Navy, and Air Force."

RMIT Monitoring

RMIT staff agreed that monitoring the implementation of RESPECT-Mil was one of the main roles of their group:

> The RMIT team is here to assist the sites to implement the RESPECT-Mil program, monitor their implementation, and to kind of manage the whole system so we can identify when people are straying away from the model and bring them back. The RMIT team monitors fidelity to the RESPECT-Mil model. We identify what is going well and what the problems are at each site.

The respondents described three main ways that they accomplished this monitoring—via performance reports, monthly site or coaching calls, and periodic site visits. This type of monitoring was seen as important. As one participant stated, "It's not an automatic that this program will make care better. If we do this wrong, we're going to make care worse."

Monitoring was perceived to be mostly effective, but some challenges were noted. In particular, respondents commented on limitations in the FIRST-STEPS data and reporting functions, including the inability to track call attempts rather than just completed encounters with service members, classifying service members' symptom levels categorically in reports rather than giving raw scores, BHCs not using the system, and the like.

One participant expressed that the program was designed with "few program standards" because "there was recognition that RESPECT-Mil was going to look different at different sites." However, "having few standards makes it difficult for fidelity monitoring."

Performance Reports

Respondents discussed performance reports and their value in monitoring. One said, "I've seen the power of data to change behavior. . . . You have to put the data in front of the folks and ask them to interpret it. . . . The coaching really helps the sites to use the information correctly."

A few respondents also noted challenges with timely data reports. They observed struggles in getting data from some clinics as well as a time lag in creating and disseminating reports: "We can only provide feedback four months down the road. We need to provide feedback in near real time." These delays in reporting resulted in offering semiannual rather than quarterly reports to the sites.

Finally, there was some discussion of the way in which information was offered back to sites. Two respondents discussed the format and tone of the reports, and the fact that they are constantly refining reports to be more user-friendly. Another respondent noted that the timing of the information is important: "Sites were getting hit with these, and they didn't feel like they were prepped for it. We've had some miscues and problems whether we send to command first or champions first. Now it goes out at the same time; they both get it and we talk on the site call about the things that will go on the reports so there are no surprises."

Monthly Site Phone Calls

Respondents also discussed monthly phone calls as a way to monitor sites and increase program fidelity. They described the content of calls changing over time, with calls early in implementation used to "talk about where are they [site staff members] in hiring, give them pointers, and see how we can help them." Once site staff are running the program, calls are used to "look at their screening data in advance of the call, see if they're on point with their reporting, anything missing, any problems." Respondents described the calls as being used for supporting sites around hiring, staff turnover, training, and space, as well as using the data to look at the overall performance and identify any issues with implementation.

Most comments about the monthly site coaching calls were positive, saying, "We let the sites know we support them" and "RMIT is involved in problem solving for sites." However, several RMIT staff members explained that the largest issue was time. As one respondent remarked, "Since we do so many calls, they take up a lot of time. . . . In addition, we have to prepare for the calls and prepare minutes afterwards."

Site Visits

Respondents described changes in their site visit procedures over time, with site visits occurring more frequently at the beginning of the original RESPECT-Mil rollout, when the RMIT team was still learning about variations in implementation. More recently, site visits have been scaled back somewhat, to just one per site, unless there are larger problems that require additional visits. In general, the site visits were described as a key way to "connect operations with the command suite" by meeting with command at the beginning and then, at the end, preparing an outbrief that reports findings. Site visits also were described as valuable for improving performance, with on respondent commenting that "usually site visits work and the program performance at the installation improves. The reported numbers get better after a site visit." However, RMIT staff described the need to cut back on site visits "because [they] are too busy and it's too expensive to visit sites frequently," and they described their exploration of other ways to connect with site commanders, such as through video teleconferencing.

Incentives

RMIT respondents were asked to discuss incentives for implementing RESPECT-Mil. Respondents explained that RMIT doesn't offer monetary incentives, but it does give awards for performance and lets sites know how they are performing in comparison with other sites. Respondents described some RCFs who also tried to set up a "competitive environment" in their clinics to encourage providers to screen service members. For example, one RCF gave out a trophy for the highest screening rate, and another presented providers with a pie chart showing the proportion of service members that each had screened.

Views on the potential effectiveness of other incentives varied. Some individuals doubted whether any incentives motivated people to improve performance or would even be allowed, while others thought that more meaningful incentives than those currently offered—such as monetary ones—would make a difference. Another respondent mentioned that there had been a push to use a relative value unit model to help incentivize behavioral health providers, but that MEDCOM didn't support it. Respondents also noted that the RMIT could use its data to reward those who have, for example, "the highest contact rate for new referrals."

Larger System Influences on RMIT

Many RMIT respondents discussed the ways that the larger military system and command structures influence the implementation of RESPECT-Mil.

Budgetary and Financial Issues

Some mentioned that budgetary and financial concerns require significant time and attention. Respondents said that alterations in the RESPECT-Mil budget or in its source budget (e.g., MEDCOM versus DCoE) affect critical implementation processes like hiring, training, and use of the FIRST-STEPS system.

Leadership Support and Buy-In

Most RMIT respondents also said that leadership support for the RESPECT-Mil program is very important for successful implementation:

> To set up operation at sites, RMIT needs command approval. RMIT works through the regional command first to coordinate points of contact at the installation level to determine who to work with and where to send the start-up kits. RMIT gives those points of contact all the program information, including training and behavioral health documents. This works well when the program is well supported by command, and does not work well if not.

Many respondents highlighted the RMCs' key role in the implementation of RESPECT-Mil. An RMIT respondent noted that coordination and collaboration with the RMCs help "push hiring forward." Those who spoke of collaboration with the RMCs said that these commands have been generally supportive and actively involved. Some RMCs have even sat in on site calls to hear "how things are going and what needs to be done to improve." Turnover is a challenge with the RMCs and other command levels, noted RMIT respondents, however: "One problem with command at every level is that the command is only there for a short amount of time—three or four years."

Big Picture Issues and the Transition to PCMH

The individuals we spoke with from the RMIT discussed the Army's transition to the PCMH model and how RESPECT-Mil and the RMIT will be affected. Some respondents talked about the increased workload associated with the expansion of services to dependents of service members, and to the Navy, Marines, and Air Force. These respondents noted that effective implementation will require careful consideration of differences between services and between civilian dependents and service members (e.g., the consequences of substance abuse).

As mentioned previously, the RMIT has already been involved in training PCMH staff, such as IBHCs.

In the transition to the PCMH model, RMIT respondents said that they expected the RMIT to play a role similar to its current one, where it is responsible for training and monitoring. However, many expressed uncertainty about how the RMIT role might evolve as the PCMH implementation progresses.

Several respondents also noted lessons learned from their experience with RESPECT-Mil, which may help facilitate the transition to and implementation of the PCMH. Some emphasized the importance of training military leaders and providers to understand and speak about the integrated model of care in order to maintain fidelity. RMIT respondents also explained that the military culture has a big impact on whether models such as RESPECT-Mil and PCMH will be accepted. For example, some talked about the way the stigma related to mental health has been a barrier to acceptance of these models. Most said that more work still needs to be done to improve the military culture's acceptance and understanding of mental health.

tronic health record. One respondent stated, "It is not overstating to say the stacks of blue forms have created a crisis of backlogged information." Respondents also noted that an advantage of integrating the screening into electronic records is the ability to avert screening fatigue. In the words of one respondent: "It's not unusual for some people to have completed ten of these screeners in a month. . . . If there were electronic records, the provider could say, 'I see you completed this last week, would you like to do this again today?'" Other respondents noted that "there should be an algorithm to avoid asking the same screener questions over and over if the answer is yes"; "people can be screened to death."

Several respondents contended that more-consistent and standardized screening is needed, particularly within specific areas. One respondent stated that screening should be "integrated into the Patient Centered Medical Home" and "many different brigades that are worthy of screening but are not (e.g., brigade combat team, [military police] brigade, signal brigade)." Another respondent noted that RESPECT-Mil "exists in MEDCOM facilities only, not in theater or in aid stations or team rooms where most patients are seen" and that "it doesn't translate into joint posts (e.g., Air Force ignores it even if they are seeing an Army patient)" and the program "needs to be in special operations, [U.S. Army Forces Command], etc."

Tracking

Many stakeholders applauded the contribution that RESPECT-Mil has made to service member care by implementing a standardized symptom tracking system (i.e., FIRST-STEPS). They indicated that the "screening tools are good," and one person recommended that behavioral health use the same tools to continue tracking service members who were screened in primary care and subsequently referred to behavioral health.

Several respondents criticized the lack of synchronization between FIRST-STEPS and AHLTA, however. They suggested that the inability to merge information from the two record systems had a negative impact on service member care. In addition, many lamented the amount of work required for staff to enter information from paper screening tools into FIRST-STEPS. A few respondents believed automating data entry rather than using paper screening tools would be more efficient: "I think that there are limitations with the FIRST-STEPS program not being automated and being labor intensive."

Staffing and Training

Several stakeholders discussed RESPECT-Mil training and staffing activities. Views on the training RESPECT-Mil provides were mixed. Some thought the training was important ("the training is a key component of RESPECT-Mil that needs to stay in place") and should be used in other settings: "The Integrated Disability Evaluation System [IDES] could potentially benefit from and use RESPECT-Mil's training program since IDES uses primary care providers to run the assessments." Others noted that there are some drawbacks to the way RESPECT-Mil trains its staff: "The centralized training is a benefit, the fact that we can send our nurses to training to use the databases and algorithms, but is also a hindrance to wait for slots to send our nurse for training though she's been here a month." Some respondents criticized the training for being "relatively superficial" and for teaching RCFs and PCPs to address only PTSD and depression, rather than "the full range of behavioral health issues."

A few stakeholders noted that the addition of RESPECT-Mil led to "workload challenges." For example, some mentioned that the program requires more support staff for effective implementation. Another recalled that when he or she was a leader at an installation starting to implement the program, "adding a program like RESPECT-Mil was an additional requirement on providers that would break the system." This stakeholder said that there was a need for more champions (e.g., BHCs, PCCs) to effectively implement RESPECT-Mil and address high demand for treatment at his or her site.

Addressing Behavioral Health Issues in Primary Care
Benefits
Respondents talked about several benefits associated with RESPECT-Mil's role in integrating behavioral health treatment within primary care settings. RESPECT-Mil was depicted as "a force multiplier within primary care, recognizing that behavioral health is short staffed" and that "evidence-based algorithms should be used to manage low-complexity behavioral health conditions with primary care resources." Another respondent stated, "The biggest challenge that that the military medical community faces is a nationwide shortage of behavioral health care specialists. . . . RESPECT-Mil helps with this issue." One respondent pointed out that "previously, behavioral health assets had been mostly in behavioral health clinics" and that RESPECT-Mil "was a great program to get behavioral health out there." Several respondents described the program's "positive impact on identifying service members with behavioral health needs who were otherwise falling under the radar." Respondents also noted that the program is "relevant in providing behavioral health training to primary care providers" and that "it also respects the reality that primary care doctors cannot do everything" and "will let primary care providers know when to refer to behavioral health specialists."

Challenges and Limitations
Respondents noted several limitations associated with the delivery of behavioral health care in primary care settings via the RESPECT-Mil program. Limitations included the lack of sufficient resources, the inability to address the full range of behavioral issues, and the lack of integration between primary care and behavioral health. One respondent stated that "RESPECT-Mil was not resourced well enough to be rolled out everywhere" and that "primary care has not been a force multiplier. . . . [They] haven't been able to take it to the level that it needed to go." Another respondent relayed that "there is a definite need for RESPECT-Mil, but . . . recruitment of more psychiatrists is needed." With respect to RESPECT-Mil's capacity to handle behavioral health issues, one respondent stated: "From a more negative perspective, sometimes service members felt like RESPECT-Mil personnel did not have enough training to address the full scope, range of behavioral health issues."

Several respondents acknowledged that "conceptually RESPECT-Mil and primary care should have always been integrated," but that "RESPECT-Mil stovepiped people" and "separate funding had been carved out for RESPECT-Mil that was different than funding for primary care, [so] the perception of integration is variable." In the words of one respondent, "It felt like it was attached to primary care like a barnacle." Another respondent remarked, "RESPECT-Mil has a medication focus, whereas behavioral clinics focus more on counseling. It would be great if we integrated these forms of treatment." As stated by a respondent, "It's like primary care and behavioral health are blind people feeling different parts of the elephant, but it's all the same elephant."

To address some of these challenges, a number of respondents underscored the importance of establishing "longitudinal relationships" between behavioral health providers and primary care providers. One respondent recommended that "behavioral health be situated parallel to primary care so there is easier access by service members and leaders" and for behavioral health to be "lined up in smaller catchment units so they can see the same provider and have continuity of care between the behavioral health team and service members."

Army Transition to PCMH and RESPECT-Mil

We asked key stakeholders about the newly created PCMH and how that would affect RESPECT-Mil. Most stakeholders agreed that RESPECT-Mil was likely to be "absorbed" or "integrated" into the PCMH model over time, and that it would likely lose its status as a separate "stovepipe" program with separate funding. Several stakeholders commented that it was a critical time to "map out how these individuals who are implementing RESPECT-Mil on a day-to-day basis in clinics are going to be utilized. Then we come up with an integrative concept plan." One stakeholder predicted that "PCMH will take care of some of the weaknesses of RESPECT-Mil," and RESPECT-Mil was noted by another as being "an essential element."

In particular, stakeholders pointed out the need for certain aspects of the RESPECT-Mil program moving forward. For instance, they explained that the screening aspect of RESPECT-Mil was important. One stakeholder observed, "The screening component needs to continue because nothing in PCMH accomplishes the same thing." However, others noted that the screening may change somewhat, with newer "electronic solutions."

Another aspect of the RESPECT-Mil program that was discussed as necessary to retain in any integration with the PCMH was the emphasis on the education of primary care physicians on medication management for depression and PTSD. For instance, one respondent mentioned that the "PCMH will have a behavioral health consultant, usually a psychologist or [licensed clinical social worker]. Medication management is a key component, and IBHCs may not bring that kind of expertise." Another stakeholder commented, "The training is a key component of RESPECT-Mil that needs to stay in place. Within the PCMH, many behavioral health consultants are not able to prescribe medication because they are psychologists and social workers. PCMH may need to work out how pharmacotherapy will work." On the other hand, several stakeholders saw the PCMH programs' embedding of behavioral health assets in primary care as augmenting RESPECT-Mil and potentially replacing the need for the BHC over time.

Third, stakeholders considered the RESPECT-Mil program's strengths in monitoring and tracking processes and outcomes was discussed to be an important aspect. One stakeholder commented that "RESPECT-Mil does seem to be light-years ahead of other programs, departments, just even because they track these things at all."

Several stakeholders commented that certain roles would need to be changed, and raised particular concerns over the RESPECT-Mil care managers and whether they could successfully shift to PCMH case manager roles.

A few stakeholders expressed that RESPECT-Mil had served its purpose already and would not be needed any longer: "At this point, RESPECT-Mil doesn't offer any component of care or system of care that isn't offered in military health care."

CHAPTER SEVEN

Discussion and Recommendations

In this concluding chapter, we provide a brief summary of the key findings of the evaluation, recommendations for improving the implementation of each of the three core components of RESPECT-Mil, and recommendations for enhancing the monitoring of program fidelity. We also discuss issues related to the implementation of collaborative care programs such as RESPECT-Mil within the military health system and the limitations of the current evaluation.

RESPECT-Mil represents one of the largest real-world undertakings to implement collaborative care for depression and PTSD on a wide scale. RESPECT-Mil has been implemented in more than 90 Army primary care clinics across 37 U.S. installations sites located all over the world. Findings indicate that RESPECT-Mil is performing in ways that are similar to other primary care collaborative care efforts that have been studied and reported on in the published scientific literature. Nonetheless, some aspects of program implementation lagged behind expectations delineated in the program design and manuals, indicating opportunities for improvement in the future. However, no other studies have been conducted in MTFs for active duty personnel, which combine aspects of primary care and employer-based care. Moreover, the majority of collaborative care studies for depression and PTSD are RCTs, which often involve a select sample of participants who are willing to consent to a research study and meet rigorous inclusion and exclusion enrollment criteria. With these caveats in mind, both the process of care and outcomes for RESPECT-Mil are generally comparable to other studies, with certain aspects of program fidelity being stronger than others. RESPECT-Mil encountered implementation barriers common to other collaborative care studies, including challenges in engaging service members to enroll and participate in the full course of recommended treatment, provider time constraints and competing demands, completion and recording of clinical assessments, turnover of organizational and clinical leaders, and provider buy-in and comfort with the program (Curran et al., 2005; Fortney, Enderle, et al., 2012; Smith et al., 2008; Thota et al., 2012; Schnurr, Friedman, Oxman, et al., 2013).

Overall, high fidelity in the implementation of routine screening for depression and PTSD was evidenced, even though there was variation across sites. Although the extent of under-reporting of depression and PTSD symptoms is unknown, a significant number of service members are positively endorsing symptoms on the brief screeners and clinical assessments. In an eight-month period, nearly 78,000 of the screened visits resulted in a positive screen on the brief depression and PTSD screening assessments. Of these positive screens, 47,797 resulted in a probable diagnosis being recorded after the administration of additional clinical assessments. During this same period, RESPECT-Mil was also responsible for facilitating 12,835 visits that resulted in accepted referrals to the program, behavioral health, and/or another psychosocial resource. Qualitative interviews with providers suggest that an even greater number of referrals to RESPECT-Mil could be facilitated if PCPs' comfort with treating depression and PTSD could be increased. It is also important to note that 8 percent of positive screens that were referred to RESPECT-Mil, behavioral health, or both were declined.

Among service members enrolled in RESPECT-Mil, a substantial proportion had no or minimal levels of depression or PTSD symptoms (16 percent) or unknown levels of presenting clinical symptom severity due to missing clinical assessments (14 percent). Further evaluation is needed to determine whether the referrals and treatment provided under RESPECT-Mil most appropriately address the needs of this set of service members. For service members with mild to severe depression and/or PTSD symptoms, a considerable proportion (38 percent) had their cases closed after the initial primary care referral and never established contact with the RCF. Twenty-one percent of service members with mild to severe depression and/or PTSD symptoms could not be engaged in or withdrew from the program. Nine percent were transferred to specialty care. Of the service members who did establish contact with RCFs, challenges were documented in procuring participation in the full course of recommend treatment, including the number of RCF follow-up contacts, treatment length, and uptake of psychotropic medication and counseling. Further, of those who had contact with an RCF, 35 percent had their cases closed because they could not be engaged in or withdrew from the program. Finally, among service members who had a follow-up clinical assessment recorded, more than a third experienced a 50 percent reduction in symptoms from baseline, and more than a fifth achieved remission.

In sum, findings highlight key junctures where opportunities for engaging service members in needed treatment for depression or PTSD may be improved. Upon referral and enrollment in RESPECT-Mil, up to one in five service members with documented mental health needs never established contact with an RCF and may have fallen through the cracks. Another fifth of service members with documented mental health needs made initial contact with an RCF but had no further follow-up contacts. This is reflective of the fact that a substantial proportion of service members who connected with RCFs were not participating in the full course of recommended treatment. Recommendations for possible areas of program improvement are summarized in the next section and are organized according to the three core components of RESPECT-Mil. In addition, we discuss recommendations related to improving the monitoring and oversight of implementation fidelity as well as issues concerning the sustainability of collaborative care programs within the larger landscape of the military health system.[1]

Recommendations to Improve the PCP and Prepared Practice Component

Screening and Assessment of Depression and PTSD

Consider ways to streamline screening and assessment. Routine screening is seen as a major strength of RESPECT-Mil. Of the total 647,642 primary care visits made during the eight-month period from August 2011 to March 2012, approximately 93 percent of these visits were screened for PTSD and depression. Though large variability was observed across Army sites, the majority of sites were screening 90 percent or more of primary care visits. PCPs cite time constraints as a major barrier to conducting screening and assessment. Potential areas where streamlining might be explored include bypassing clinical assessments among service mem-

---

[1]   A crosswalk between the recommendations and study findings are provided in Appendix N.

bers who have been recently screened and diagnosed by the program, finding ways to ease the administrative burden involved in conducting and recording assessments, and forgoing screening among service members already enrolled in RESPECT-Mil.

Determine the value of screening service members already enrolled in behavioral health care. Half of the positive screens were documented as already being followed in behavioral health and no referral was issued. Flagging service members who are experiencing clinically significant depression and/or PTSD symptoms despite being followed in behavioral health may provide an opportunity to intervene to ensure that adequate levels of treatment are being obtained. Service members may benefit from a referral to RESPECT-Mil, where RCFs can assess and support engagement in recommended treatments for depression and PTSD and track symptom change in response to treatment.

Mitigate disruptions due to staff turnover. Unlike civilian settings, military installations are subject to regular staff turnover due to deployments, permanent change of station moves, and separations from military service. Army sites varied in how staff disruptions were managed, with some sites being significantly affected in their ability to maintain fidelity to the RESPECT-Mil program. To stabilize the implementation fidelity of RESPECT-Mil over time and during periods of staff turnover, consider establishing ongoing training and peer mentoring within the program.

Enhance command support. Due to the use of different screening and diagnostic instruments as well as scoring algorithms in other research studies, there are no comparable benchmarks to accurately gauge whether service members are underreporting on RESPECT-Mil screening and diagnostic assessments. However, concerns regarding the underreporting of PTSD and depression symptoms due to stigma have been well documented (Institute of Medicine, 2012). Findings from stakeholder and RESPECT-Mil provider discussions indicate that service members may not report PTSD and depression symptoms during routine screening because of anticipated negative repercussions from their fellow service members and commanders. Continuing and enhancing command support for the RESPECT-Mil program, as well as other evidence-based programs for psychological health, may foster greater openness and disclosure of PTSD and depression among service members.

Explore expanding routine screening and evidence-based primary care management practices for depression and PTSD beyond MTFs. During the eight-month study period, 2 percent of total screened visits (i.e., 12,835 primary care visits) resulted in a referral to mental health treatment. Even though the degree to which service members may be underreporting symptoms during routine screening is unknown, findings indicate that RESPECT-Mil is catching people who may have fallen through the cracks. Stakeholders and RESPECT-Mil providers recommended that routine screening for PTSD and depression be expanded to all primary care settings, including in theater, aid stations, team rooms, joint posts, special ops, and U.S. Army Forces Command. However, given that research indicates that screening alone may not influence clinical outcomes (Institute of Medicine, 2012; O'Connor et al., 2009), considering the implementation of routine screening in other types of primary care settings should go hand in hand with considering the implementation of evidence-based primary care management practices of depression and PTSD.

Referral and Management of Depression and PTSD

Increase PCP engagement and comfort. RESPECT-Mil provider discussions revealed that some PCPs may not feel comfortable with managing the mental health needs of service members in primary care. Identified concerns include fears related to being held liable for adverse behavioral health outcomes and beliefs that PTSD should be handled in behavioral health. Ways to increase PCPs' engagement in the program and comfort with addressing behavioral health needs could include monitoring individual PCP performance, providing additional training with PCCs, and strengthening the consultative relationship with BHCs, as well as structural or cultural changes to the primary care environment that might facilitate the time and effort needed to address mental health issues in primary care.

Incentivize and support primary care champions. PCCs have severe constraints on their time and need to demonstrate productivity outside the RESPECT-Mil program. Explore opportunities to incentivize, recognize, and support those in the champion positions so that they can continue to train, monitor, and assist PCPs in retaining fidelity to the program.

Consider whether modifications are needed given the mix of service members referred to the program. Of the service members referred and enrolled into RESPECT-Mil, less than half met full the criteria for depression or PTSD. Another quarter had mild to moderate symptoms. Including service members who do not meet full the criteria for a probable diagnosis but experience mild to moderate symptoms may be appropriate given that subthreshold levels of depression and PTSD can be associated with significant psychosocial impairment. A fifth of service members had no or minimal depression or PTSD symptoms. Further investigation is needed to understand the reasons for the referral and enrollment of these service members and whether there are any associated clinical benefits with this practice.

Recommendations to Improve the RCF Component

Use field experiences with shorter and less intensive services to update and expand RESPECT-Mil manuals. Processes of care in RESPECT-Mil are comparable to some civilian and VA studies but less intensive than outlined in the RESPECT-Mil manuals and training. Thus, there is currently a mismatch between RESPECT-Mil program protocol and RCFs' ability to engage service members in the recommended treatment intensity and duration. A recent metaanalytic review of collaborative care programs for depression concluded that further research is needed to identify the optimal frequency and intensity of care management sessions and whether additional sessions in cases of treatment nonresponse are beneficial (Thota et al., 2012). Another metaanalytic review found no relationship between the treatment-effect size and the duration and number of case management sessions (Gilbody et al., 2006). If service member engagement in treatment cannot be enhanced, consider ways to adapt the program to maximize the fewer visits and shorter timeline that have been more characteristic of a substantial proportion of program participants.

Strengthen the handoff between the PCP and the RCF. A significant proportion of service members (38 percent) who are referred to the program never establish contact with an RCF. More than half of these service members either withdrew from the program or could not be engaged or contacted. Explore strategies to address service member dropout after the initial primary care referral, including training PCPs to better orient and introduce service members to the program as well as providing warm handoffs within clinics. PCPs have been found to miss potential opportunities to address mental health issues with patients and may benefit from ongoing training that extends beyond medication management (Tai-Seale et al., 2010).

Facilitate engagement and communication with service members. Service members with mild to severe depression and/or PTSD who successfully establish their initial contact with RCFs have a mean of 2.6 subsequent follow-ups with RCFs and remain enrolled in the program for a mean of 57 days. Moreover, during the period of enrollment in the program, only 46 percent of service members reported starting any medication or counseling. Given that the level of treatment engagement is below optimal for a substantial proportion of service members, strategies for facilitating engagement and communication should be explored. This may include the use of newer technologies for communication (e.g., texting, social media), as well training RCFs in motivational interviewing strategies.

Enlist command in support of service members' treatment engagement and adherence while recognizing that some service members may want to keep their treatment confidential. According to provider and stakeholder discussions, barriers to treatment engagement include service members' concerns about the potential negative repercussions on job performance and career advancement, as well as the lack of flexibility and support on the part of commanders to accommodate treatment requirements (e.g., modifying schedules to attend treatment appointments or to adjust to medication side effects). Enlisting the support of commanders could play an integral role in creating incentives for service members to engage in and adhere to treatment. Potential avenues to explore could include training commanders on the potential impact of policies that may discourage treatment seeking among service members, building collaborative relationships between commanders and PCPs, and promoting commander awareness of the program via trainings delivered by BHCs or PCCs.

Fortify communication between providers. Based on provider discussions, several areas of communication between providers were identified as possible targets for improvement. To strengthen the coordination of care among providers, the following could be considered: explore ways to integrate and streamline record management systems (e.g., AHLTA, FIRST-STEPS), expand venues for communication outside the medical record systems (e.g., colocation, cross-unit meetings focused on service member care), and identify strategies to ensure that PCPs are obtaining feedback (positive and negative) about the service members they have referred to RESPECT-Mil.

Recommendations to Improve the BHC Component

Ensure that the BHC role is adequately supported. Barriers to carrying out BHC responsibilities include severe constraints on staff time, competing priorities related to their primary occupational responsibilities within behavioral health, and few incentives to participate in RESPECT-Mil. To ensure that BHCs can perform optimally, consider ways to provide adequate and protected time for RESPECT-Mil duties, incentivize participation in the program, and ensure efficient staffing of cases.

Consider enhancing the BHC role. BHCs were depicted as functioning positively in their role as informal consultants to PCPs about the diagnosis and management of depression and PTSD. Consideration might be given to enhancing the BHC role in providing more-intensive support to PCPs. Expansion of the BHC role may occur through changes in location, availability, and incentives. BHCs' engagement may be especially important during the initial phases of implementation, when PCPs are being trained in the program and their comfort and skill levels in managing behavioral health issues are developing.

Recommendations to Improve Monitoring

Under the order of the U.S. Army Medical Command, RMIT was created to oversee and monitor the implementation of RESPECT-Mil across all designated sites. At the provider level, views on monitoring were mixed, with varying levels of reported awareness and direct interaction with RMIT monitoring activities. The perceived effectiveness of RMIT monitoring activities, such as site calls, site visits, and performance reports, also varied.

Augment individualized and real-time performance feedback. Currently, no apparent, routinized protocol is in place to provide PCPs with performance feedback on fidelity to the program. RESPECT-Mil RCFs and administrative assistants were described as informal monitors and informants to PCCs, who would address PCP noncompliance. PCP performance indicators could include the monitoring of appropriate mental health screening and referral, rates of successful handoffs to RCFs, adherence to recommended medication treatment guidelines, and timely follow-up appointments. Similarly, a system for monitoring and providing feedback about BHC performance does not appear to be established. BHC performance indicators could include monitoring whether treatment nonresponse, medication side effects, and treatment nonadherence are being appropriately handled. FIRST-STEPS is a system through which RCF performance can be monitored, but the type and frequency of feedback provided is unclear. Also, the optimal caseload capacity for care facilitators did not appear to be clearly determined or conveyed. Patient panels for care facilitators have ranged from 143 to 165 in other depression collaborative care studies (Liu et al., 2007). Performance feedback for RCFs could include the rate at which service members are being successfully connected to medication and counseling, engaging in the full course of recommended treatment, and appropriately referred to other behavioral resources. FIRST-STEPS may be a platform through which provider performance can be tracked and monitored with individualized, real-time feedback if individual-level data can be made accessible. Development of targets for optimal performance will also be important so that sites can gauge their own performance against target metrics.

Create incentives for sites and providers to buy in to quality improvement processes. More routine, localized, on-site monitoring may increase ownership and investment in quality improvement processes. In addition, localized monitoring may facilitate more real-time and personalized feedback, which is more challenging to conduct when the monitoring of all Army sites is centralized.

Continue support for RMIT or similar centralized quality improvement programs. The RMIT data collection efforts on clinic screening and referral practices and care management activities via FIRST-STEPS allow for valuable tracking of implementation fidelity as well as program effectiveness. This is in line with one of the major recommendations issued in a 2012 Institute of Medicine report, *Treatment for Posttraumatic Stress Disorder in Military and Veteran Populations*, which called for DoD and the VA to "institute programs of research that evaluate the efficacy, effectiveness, and implementation of all their PTSD screening, treatment, and rehabilitation services" (Institute of Medicine, 2012, p. 13). A more recent 2014 Institute of Medicine report underscored the importance of having a performance management system to track PTSD clinical outcomes and program quality indicators (Institute of Medicine, 2014).

Establish an RMIT self-monitoring process. Ongoing evaluations of the relative merit and aspects of different monitoring strategies may be beneficial in targeting which activities should be continued and supported, particularly in light of limited resources.

Implementation of RESPECT-Mil Within the Military Health System

With the rollout of the PCMH, careful consideration is needed to determine which aspects of RESPECT-Mil add value and can be preserved. Continued monitoring and oversight of the RESPECT-Mil program and the PCMH will be necessary as these programs change and adapt over time, since they have similar goals but different structural elements. Careful attention is also advised on how the evidence-based routines and practices encompassed by RESPECT-Mil can be maintained given existing challenges to maintaining fidelity to the 3CM. This is particularly important in light of the anticipated added responsibilities that accompany the implementation of the PCMH.

Regardless of which form the resulting program takes, lessons from the RESPECT-Mil implementation suggest that the role of command leadership and installation policies are crucial in the success of behavioral interventions in primary care. Significant reluctance for admitting problems and seeking care are noted within the RESPECT-Mil program despite its reduction in barriers and routine screening, and our analysis also points to policies and procedures in place that make it difficult to reach service members or for them to attend routine appointments in some settings. Strong encouragement and messaging that seeking mental health care is a sign of strength and valued by the Army will be an important element of all efforts moving forward to integrate behavioral and primary care.

From the RMIT perspective, it was also clear that installation commands and RMCs have the ability to facilitate or interfere with program implementation. For any programs rolled out in military clinical settings in the short and long term, lessons from RESPECT-Mil indicate that garnering support from RMCs and installation commands is critical. Lack of support from organizational leaders has been identified as a key barrier to implementing collaborative care programs (Fortney, Pyne, Smith, et al., 2009; Smith et al., 2008). Discussions with key leadership in the military health system indicated a valuing of the screening component of RESPECT-Mil but less familiarity with components targeting the effective management of behavioral health problems in primary care. For this reason, implementation teams such as the RMIT should consider strategically engaging and selecting leadership who are invested in the program, and who have the skills needed to effectively network and facilitate outreach to multiple levels of command.

Limitations

This implementation evaluation had the following key aims: (1) assess the degree to which RESPECT-Mil is being implemented in Army primary care settings; (2) identify facilitators and barriers to the implementation of RESPECT-Mil; and (3) examine the sustainability of RESPECT-Mil from the perspective of key stakeholders within the military health system. Beyond the scope of this present evaluation were other potentially important RESPECT-Mil implementation indicators that would have further tapped into the quality of care that is being delivered through the program. For example, further study is needed to examine whether the optimal psychotropic medication algorithms were being prescribed and whether service members were being engaged in evidence-based psychotherapy. Examining the process of care for service members exhibiting suicidal risk was also outside the purview of the current evaluation. In addition, given that this evaluation could not employ a randomized controlled or quasi-experimental study design because RESPECT-Mil was already implemented at most installations, conclusions about the efficacy of RESPECT-Mil beyond treatment as usual is limited. Analyses related to the efficacy of RESPECT-Mil were also hindered by the fact that treatment outcomes could only be examined among the subset of service members who had established contact with an RCF and had at least one follow-up assessment recorded. Further, given that Army primary care clinics did not routinely screen and track depression and PTSD symptoms, we were unable to compare treatment outcomes across sites that had implemented RESPECT-Mil versus sites than had not yet implemented the program. Limitations with respect to the adoption indicators used in this study should also be noted. Levels of program adoption across sites were examined only for screening and referral rates. The adoption of other key components of RESPECT-Mil (e.g., RCF contacts) across sites warrants additional examination. Finally, the influence of organizational factors (e.g., installation size, colocation with other service branches, site leadership) on the implementation of RESPECT-Mil could not be explored extensively.

Findings from analyses of FIRST-STEPS data should be interpreted cautiously. Given that FIRST-STEPS was designed for use as an electronic case-management tracking tool, there are a number of limitations inherent in using these data to assess the implementation of RESPECT-Mil. First, these data only contain information that providers remembered to document. To the extent that providers neglected to input every encounter and service delivered, we may have underestimated levels of program fidelity. Moreover, we were unable to determine the degree to which missing FIRST-STEPS data and variables such as time between assessments were results of provider (non)adherence to the RESPECT-Mil protocol or of patient (non)adherence to the program. Further, our measures of implementation were limited to the types of information collected in the Monthly Screening and Referral Clinic Reports and FIRST-STEPS. The use of measures specifically developed to assess program fidelity may have provided more-accurate indicators of implementation (see, e.g., Oxman et al., 2006). In fact, both the FIRST-STEPS and qualitative data provide relatively limited information about providers' fidelity to the program. Unfortunately, this study and others like it suffer from a dearth of well-developed criteria and measures for evaluating primary care–based behavioral health treatment (Institute of Medicine, 2012). Future research should focus on developing and improving measures and should use data collection strategies that rely less on the reports of busy providers, such as having trained observers code fidelity to RESPECT-Mil. Finally, data aggregated at the installation level do not capture variation at the provider level, such as differences in RCFs' and BHCs' implementation of the program. We were able to draw some comparisons between providers with our qualitative data, but these data are only representative of the subset of sites that we sampled and may not be generalizable to other MTFs.

For the qualitative portion of the evaluation, we sampled sites according to their level of implementation (according to clinic data) and site characteristics, such as size, in order to maximize variability in responses. Response rates were good, and we used a standard set of discussion questions. Despite these methodological strengths, it is important to note that the views of participating providers are not necessarily representative of all providers engaged with RESPECT-Mil. Similarly, the views of the military health leaders (key stakeholders) we spoke with may not be generalizable. In fact, many of the participating key stakeholders might be assigned to a different post by the time this report is published, given the high rate of turnover of military leadership. New leadership may have different views and will have the power to change policies accordingly. One of the ultimate goals of this evaluation is to inform these new leaders of the lessons learned from RESPECT-Mil in order to improve policies related to the behavioral health of service members in the future.

Conclusions

The real-world implementation of RESPECT-Mil in Army primary care settings is achieving results that are comparable to other collaborative care efforts that are often conducted under more tightly controlled research conditions. As with other collaborative care efforts, RESPECT-Mil encountered significant implementation barriers. Challenges included establishing initial contact with service members upon referral to the program, procuring service member engagement in the full course of recommended treatment, obtaining provider buy-in, provider time constraints and competing demands, and the provision of oversight and accountability to program fidelity. Factors that facilitated the implementation of RESPECT-Mil included perceptions of routine screening for depression and PTSD as a valuable means for reaching service members who may fall through the cracks; BHC support and consultation to PCPs; and the solid linkages between PCPs and RCFs. Findings highlight key junctures where opportunities for engaging service members in needed treatment for depression or PTSD may be improved. Potential avenues for improving program fidelity include increasing PCPs' comfort and incentives to address depression and PTSD within primary care settings, ensuring warm handoffs between the initial primary care referral to the care facilitator in order to protect against dropouts, equipping providers with additional skills and strategies to improve treatment engagement, and providing individualized provider performance feedback. Even if perfect program fidelity were achieved, barriers such as stigma or lack of leadership support for recommended treatment plans are unlikely to be completely overcome without corresponding shifts in increased organizational and policy support. Recommendations issued in this report on how to improve the implementation of collaborative care programs aimed at enhancing mental health care within primary care are targeted at the provider, clinic administration, and military organizational levels. Recommendations are relevant to current efforts under way to usher in the PCMH by building on the foundations and infrastructure developed by RESPECT-Mil.

Department of Defense MEDCOM Form 774

MEDICAL RECORD - RESPECT-Mil PRIMARY CARE SCREENING	
For use of this form, see MEDCOM Circular 40-20; the proponent agency is Office of The Surgeon General	**TODAY'S DATE:** _____

Please check the best answer to each of the questions on this page. Enter your personal information at the bottom and return this page to the medic or nurse.

SECTION I

Over the **LAST 2 WEEKS,** have you been bothered by any of the following problems?

1. Feeling down, depressed, or hopeless. ☐ Yes ☐ No

2. Little interest or pleasure in doing things. ☐ Yes ☐ No

SECTION II

Have you had any experience that was so frightening, horrible, or upsetting that **IN THE PAST MONTH,** you...

3. Had any nightmares about it or thought about it when you did not want to? ☐ Yes ☐ No

4. Tried hard not to think about it or went out of your way to avoid situations that remind you of it? ☐ Yes ☐ No

5. Were constantly on guard, watchful, or easily startled? ☐ Yes ☐ No

6. Felt numb or detached from others, activities, or your surroundings? ☐ Yes ☐ No

FOR OFFICIAL USE ONLY

PATIENT IDENTIFICATION *(Please print.)*:

NAME (Last, First, MI): _____

DOB: ____ / ____ / ____ Unit _____

Rank: _____ SSN: *(Please enter last 4 of SSN.)*: _____

Phone: (Home/Cell): _____

(Unit/Work): _____

MEDCOM FORM 774, OCT 2010 PREVIOUS EDITION MAY BE USED UNTIL EXHAUSTED Page 1 of 2
MC v3.01

PROVIDER ASSESSMENT - (overflow to other side; sign & date entries below)

SECTION I: RESPECT - Mil SCREENING RESULTS -   (check all that apply)

☐ Depression & PTSD Screens BOTH NEGATIVE ------- STOP / DONE unless otherwise indicated
☐ Depression Screen POSITIVE (1 or more of Items # 1 - 2 marked 'YES') ----- Score PHQ-9 + SUICIDE RISK 1.i
☐ PTSD Screen POSITIVE (2 or more of Items # 3-6 marked 'YES') --------- Score PCL + SUICIDE RISK 19

SCREEN / SYMPTOM ASSESSMENT:

PHQ-9 Score: _____   **Risk Item 1.i:** _____

PCL Score: _____   **Risk Item 19:** _____

SECTION II: POSITIVE SUICIDE RISK SCREEN

IF PHQ-9 OR PCL RISK ITEM(S) IS POSITIVE, assess suicide risk history, social support, substance use, and note whether ideas are active, current, or involve planning, feasible intent.

THEN RATE & DOCUMENT SUICIDE RISK:

☐ LOW
☐ INTERMED
☐ HIGH

SECTION III: DIAGNOSIS - (check all that apply)

☐ Possible PTSD (Code 300.00, Anxiety Disorder NOS)   ☐ False Positive Screen (No Depression or PTSD present)
☐ PTSD (Code 309.81)   ☐ Other Diagnoses:
☐ Depression (Code 311)

SECTION IV: TREATMENT PLAN

List med changes, counseling, follow-up, and other

Offer depression/PTSD education materials

SECTION V: DISPOSITION PLAN - (check all that apply)

REFERRAL MADE TO ▼	▼ **NO REFERRAL MADE BECAUSE**
RESPECT-Mil ☐	☐ No Behavioral Health treatment need identified
A Behavioral Health Specialist ☐	☐ Behavioral Health need will be addressed in primary care
Another psychosocial resource (describe) ☐	☐ RESPECT-Mil declined
	☐ Behavioral Health Specialist referral declined
	☐ Already followed in RESPECT-Mil
	☐ Already followed by Behavioral Health Specialist
	☐ Already followed by another psychosocial resource describe

Provider (sign & stamp):   Date _____

Patient Health Questionnaire-9 (PHQ-9) for Depression

Over the *last 2 weeks*, how often have you been bothered by any of the following problems?

		Not at all	Several days	More than half the days	Nearly every day
1	Little interest or pleasure in doing things	0	1	2	3
2	Feeling down, depressed, or hopeless	0	1	2	3
3	Trouble falling or staying asleep, or sleeping too much	0	1	2	3
4	Feeling tired or having little energy	0	1	2	3
5	Poor appetite or overeating	0	1	2	3
6	Feeling bad about yourself—or that you are a failure or have let yourself or your family down	0	1	2	3
7	Trouble concentrating on things, such as reading the newspaper or watching television	0	1	2	3
8	Moving or speaking so slowly that other people could have noticed. Or the opposite—being so fidgety or restless that you have been moving around a lot more than usual	0	1	2	3
9	Thought that you would be better off dead, or of hurting yourself in some way	0	1	2	3
10	If you checked off any problems, how difficult have those problems made it for you to do your work, take care of things at home, or get along with other people?	Not difficult at all _____ Somewhat difficult _____ Very difficult _____ Extremely difficult _____			

RESPECT-Mil Scoring for PHQ-9 for Depression

Criteria for Establishing a Tentative Diagnosis of Depression

- Each of the questions represents a system (per the *DSM-IV*). Therefore, the maximum symptom count possible is nine.
- One of the first two questions should be endorsed at two to three points for a diagnosis of depression.
- Responses to questions one through eight of "more than half the days" (two points) *or* "nearly every day" (three points) count as a symptom. *One symptom per question.*
- The *exception* is question number nine, which evaluates suicidal ideation. Any response other than "not at all" (zero points) counts as a symptom.
- A total of five or more symptoms must be endorsed as at least "several days," and question 10 (functional impairment) must be endorsed as at least "somewhat difficult" or greater.

Calculating the PHQ-9 Severity Score

- A total depression severity score is obtained by summing the values of all endorsed responses.
- A PHQ-9 severity score can range from 0 to a maximum of 27 points.

  Table C.1 presents the provisional diagnoses and treatment options based on these scores.

Table C.1
Provisional Diagnoses and Treatment Options Based on PHQ-9 Severity Scores

PHQ-9 Score	Provisional Diagnosis	Treatment Options
0–4	No depression	N/A
5–9	Minimal symptoms[a]	Support, educate to call if worse; return in one month
10–14	Minor depression[b]	Support, watchful waiting
	Dysthymia[c]	Antidepressant or psychotherapy
	Major depression, mild	Antidepressant or psychotherapy
15–19	Major depression, moderately severe	Antidepressant or psychotherapy
> 20	Major depression, severe	Antidepressant *and* psychotherapy (especially if not improved on monotherapy)

[a] If symptoms have been present for more than two years, then the diagnosis is probable chronic depression, which warrants antidepressants or psychotherapy. (Ask, "In the past two years, have you felt depressed or sad most days, even if you felt okay sometimes?")

[b] If symptoms have been present for more than one month or severe functional impairment, consider active treatment.

[c] If symptoms have been present for more than two years, then the diagnosis is probable chronic depression, which warrants antidepressants or psychotherapy. (Ask, "In the past two years, have you felt depressed or sad most days, even if you felt okay sometimes?")

PTSD Checklist (PCL)

		Response:	Not at all	A little bit	Moderately	Quite a bit	Extremely
One	1	Repeated, disturbing memories, thoughts, or images of a stressful experience from the past?	0	1	2	3	4
	2	Repeated, disturbing dreams of a stressful experience from the past?	0	1	2	3	4
	3	Suddenly acting or feeling as if a stressful experience were happening again (as if you were reliving it)?	0	1	2	3	4
	4	Feeling very upset when something reminded you of a stressful experience from the past?	0	1	2	3	4
	5	Having physical reactions (e.g., heart pounding, trouble breathing, or sweating) when something reminded you of a stressful experience from the past?	0	1	2	3	4
Three	6	Avoid thinking about or talking about a stressful experience from the past or avoid having feelings related to it?	0	1	2	3	4
	7	Avoid activities or situations because they remind you of a stressful experience from the past?	0	1	2	3	4
	8	Trouble remembering important parts of a stressful experience from the past?	0	1	2	3	4
	9	Loss of interest in things that you used to enjoy?	0	1	2	3	4
	10	Feeling distant or cut off from other people?	0	1	2	3	4
	11	Feeling emotionally numb or being unable to have loving feelings for those close to you?	0	1	2	3	4
	12	Feeling as if your future will somehow be cut short?	0	1	2	3	4
Two	13	Trouble falling or staying asleep?	0	1	2	3	4
	14	Feeling irritable or having angry outbursts?	0	1	2	3	4
	15	Having difficulty concentrating	0	1	2	3	4
	16	Being "super alert" or watchful and on guard?	0	1	2	3	4
	17	Feeling jumpy or easily startled?	0	1	2	3	4

Suicide risk and functional impairment questions (not included in symptom count or severity score)

---

18 If you checked off any of the above problems, how difficult have these problems made it for you to do your work, take care of things at home, or get along with other people?

_____ Not difficult _____ Somewhat difficult _____ Very difficult _____ Extremely difficult

19 During the last 2 weeks have you had thoughts that you would be better off dead, or hurting yourself in some way?

_____ Yes _____ No

If "Yes," how often? _____ Several days _____ More than half the days _____ Almost every day

---

NOTE: Based on the number of symptoms rated at least a moderately severe level (≥ 3) in each of the three categories (intrusion, ≥ 1 symptom endorsed; avoidance, ≥ 3 symptoms endorsed; hyperarousal ≥ 2 symptoms endorsed) in the past month, a total severity score > 13, and the presence of functional impairment, the PCC can formulate a working PTSD diagnosis.

RESPECT-Mil Scoring for PTSD Checklist (PCL)

Criteria for Establishing a Tentative Diagnosis of PTSD

- Each question (1–17) represents a symptom per the DSM-IV.
- A symptom is counted when the question is endorsed as "moderately," "quite a bit," or "extremely" bothersome.
- Within each symptom category (intrusion, avoidance, arousal) there are a minimum number of symptoms with a score of at least 3 (moderately bothered) that are required to substantiate a diagnosis (see Table E.1).
- A total PTSD severity score is obtained from PCL by summing the values of all endorsed responses.
- The minimum PCL score is 0 and the maximum score is 68.

Provisional PTSD Diagnosis Based on PCL Scores

Based on the number of symptoms present at least at a moderate level (≥ 2) in each of the three categories (intrusion, avoidance, and arousal) in the past month, with a total score of > 13, plus the presence of functional impairment, a working PTSD diagnosis can be formulated.

Calculating the PCL Severity Score

See Table E.2 for how to calculate the PCL severity score.

Table E.1
Minimum Endorsement per Symptom Category for Diagnosis

Category	Minimum Endorsement
Intrusion	1 out of 5 questions in category
Avoidance	3 out of 7 questions in category
Arousal	2 out of 5 questions in category
TOTAL SYMPTOMS	6 of 17 questions by categories noted above

Table E.2
PCL Severity Score

PCL Symptoms and Impairment	PCL Severity	Provisional Diagnosis	Treatment Recommendations
< 6 symptoms at moderate or greater severity, but no functional impairment	< 13	Subthreshold or no PTSD	• Reassurance and/or supportive counseling • Education • Self-management activity
≥ 6 symptoms at moderate or greater severity (≥ 1 intrusion symptom, ≤ 3 avoidance symptoms, and ≥ 2 hyperarousal symptoms, plus functional impairment)	13–32	PTSD, mild	• SSRI • Self-management activity
	≥ 33	PTSD, moderate to severe	• If no improvement after 12 weeks, refer for cognitive behavioral therapy • Specialty referral[a]

[a] Refer for comanagement with a behavioral health specialist if patient is:
  • High suicide risk,
  • Has substance abuse,
  • Has complex psychosocial needs, and/or
  • Other active behavioral disorders (except depression).

Stage-by-Topic Discussion Protocol for RESPECT-Mil Behavioral Health Champions

Opening questions:
- How long have you been working with RESPECT-Mil?
- How long at this current site?
- What has been your overall experience with RESPECT-Mil?
- What's useful?
- What's not useful?

The next questions are about your role and responsibilities within RESPECT-Mil.

		Roles/Responsibilities	Implementation	Monitoring	Barriers/Facilitators

Initial Patient Encounter		• Let's start with the initial patient staffing calls.
		• What's your role in:
		  - Treatment planning?
		  - Addressing treatment barriers (e.g., treatment will hurt their career; don't need treatment; meds. are addictive; side effects)?
		• How are these processes the same or different for PTSD vs. depression?
			• You've told me what you do during the initial patient staffing calls; how does this fit with what is prescribed by the RESPECT-Mil program?
			• How effective is RESPECT-Mil in facilitating the initial staffing for cases?
			• In what ways is RESPECT-Mil *not* working?
				• How is your implementation of the initial patient staffing calls monitored (if at all)?
				• How is the information from the monitoring process used to identify problems or improve performance?
					• What prevents you from being able to carry out your role and responsibilities?
					• What would help you to carry out your responsibilities better during the initial staffing of cases?
					• Other recommendations?

Monitoring Patients		• What are your responsibilities after the initial patient staffing call?
		• What is your role, if any, in addressing:
		  - Treatment nonadherence?
		  - Unresponsiveness to treatment?
		  - Side effects?
		• How do you know what happens to patients after the initial patient staffing call?
			• You've told me some of the things you do after the initial patient staffing calls; how does this fit with what is prescribed by the RESPECT-Mil program?
			• How effective is RESPECT-Mil in monitoring and addressing problems that arise in treatment plans?
			• What has *not* been effective?
				• How is your role in caring for patients after the initial patient staffing call being monitored?
				• How is the information from the monitoring process used to identify problems or improve performance?
					• What would help you to monitor patients better after the initial patient staffing call?
					• How can you be better supported to address treatment nonadherence, unresponsiveness, and side effects?
					• Other recommendations?

Now I'm going to ask you about the coordination of care among providers.

	Roles/Responsibilities	Implementation	Monitoring	Barriers/Facilitators
Coordination	• What is your role in coordinating care with CFs [care facilitators]? • What information do you provide to and receive from CFs? • How is information exchanged?	• How does the coordination of care that you described fit with what is prescribed by RESPECT-Mil? • How effective is RESPECT-Mil in facilitating the coordination of care between PCPs, CFs, and BHCs? • What hasn't been effective?	• How is coordination of care monitored? • How is information from the monitoring process used to identify problems or improve performance?	• What would facilitate better coordination of care between PCPs, CFs, and BHCs? • Other recommendations?

Closing questions:
- Given all the various roles and responsibilities discussed, what happens when there is staff turnover (e.g., permanent change of station, deployment)? Any preparations in place?
- What has been the impact on the traditional behavioral health care system?
- How is RESPECT-Mil similar or different from other behavioral health initiatives such as the Patient Centered Medical Home?
- In your opinion, what needs to change the most in the way that the military health system addresses the behavioral health concerns of service members?

Stage-by-Topic Discussion Protocol for RESPECT-Mil Nurse Care Facilitators

Opening questions:
- How long have you been working with RESPECT-Mil?
- How long at this current site?
- What has been your overall experience with RESPECT-Mil?
- What's useful?
- What's not useful?

The next questions are about your role and responsibilities in RESPECT-Mil. We'll be talking about 3 different components: the initial 1-week follow-up visit, monitoring patients after the 1-week follow-up visit, and the coordination of care among providers.

	Roles/Responsibilities	Implementation	Monitoring	Barriers/Facilitators
Initial Patient Encounter	• First, what are your roles and responsibilities with respect to: - the 1-week follow-up visit with patients referred to RESPECT-Mil? - treatment planning? - addressing treatment barriers (e.g., treatment will hurt their career; don't need treatment; meds. are addictive; side effects)? • How are these processes the same or different for PTSD vs. depression?	• You've told me what you do during the 1-week follow-up visit; how does this fit with what is prescribed by the RESPECT-Mil program? • How effective is RESPECT-Mil in: - identifying PTSD or depression? - facilitating access to mental health treatment? - addressing treatment barriers? • In what ways is RESPECT-Mil *not* working?	• How are your responsibilities for the 1-week follow-up visit monitored (if at all)? • How is the information from the monitoring process used to identify problems or improve performance? • How useful is the info?	• What prevents you from being able to carry out your role and responsibilities? • What would help you to carry out your responsibilities better with respect to the 1-week follow-up visit? • Other recommendations?
Monitoring Patients	• How do you stay in contact with patients after the 1-week follow-up visit? • What's your role, if any, in addressing: - treatment nonadherence? - unresponsiveness to treatment? - side effects? • How do you know when patients are having problems with the behavioral health treatment plan?	• How does what you do after the 1-week follow-up visit fit with what is prescribed by the RESPECT-Mil program? • How effective is RESPECT-Mil in monitoring patients and in addressing problems that arise in treatment? • What is *not* working?	• How is your role in caring for patients after the 1-week follow-up visit monitored? • How is the information from the monitoring process used to identify problems or improve performance?	• How can you be better supported in caring for patients after the 1-week follow-up visit? • How can you be better supported to address treatment nonadherence, unresponsiveness, and side effects? • Other recommendations?

Now I'm going to ask you about the coordination of care among providers.

	Roles/Responsibilities	Implementation	Monitoring	Barriers/Facilitators
Coordination	• What is your role in coordinating care with providers? • What information do you provide to and receive from PCPs? • What information do you provide to and receive from BHCs? • How is information exchanged?	• How does the coordination of care that you described fit with what is prescribed by RESPECT-Mil? • How effective is RESPECT-Mil in facilitating the coordination of care between PCPs, CFs, and BHCs? • What has not been effective?	• How is coordination of care monitored? • How is information from the monitoring process used to identify problems or improve performance?	• What would facilitate better coordination of care between PCPs, CFs, and BHCs? • Other recommendations?

Closing questions:
- Given all the various roles and responsibilities discussed, what happens when there is staff turnover (e.g., permanent change of station, deployment)? Any preparations in place?
- How has RESPECT-Mil affected patient care?
- How is RESPECT-Mil similar or different from other behavioral health initiatives such as the Patient Centered Medical Home?
- In your opinion, what needs to change the most in the way that the military health system addresses the behavioral health concerns of service members?
- Ask RCF to nominate the best- and worst-performing primary care provider with respect to implementation of the RESPECT-Mil program.

Stage-by-Topic Discussion Protocol for RESPECT-Mil Primary Care Champions

Opening questions:
- How long have you been working with RESPECT-Mil?
- How long at this current site?
- What has been your overall experience with RESPECT-Mil?
- What's useful?
- What's not useful?

The next questions are about your activities around caring for patients with PTSD or depression. We'll be talking about 3 different components: the initial patient encounter, monitoring patients, and coordination of care.

	Roles/Responsibilities	Implementation	Monitoring	Barriers/Facilitators
Initial Patient Encounter	• Let's start with the initial patient encounter. • What is the primary care provider's role (if any) in: - the identification of PTSD or depression? - treatment referrals (to RESPECT-Mil)? - how treatment barriers are handled (e.g., treatment will hurt their career; don't need treatment; meds. are addictive; side effects)? • How is this process the same or different for patients with PTSD vs. depression? • What is your role in ensuring that PCPs carry out these responsibilities?	• How effective is RESPECT-Mil in facilitating: the identification of PTSD and depression? • access to mental health treatment? • responsiveness to treatment barriers? • In what ways is RESPECT-Mil *not* working? • In what ways is it working?	• How are PCPs monitored (if at all) with respect to their RESPECT-Mil responsibilities during the initial patient encounter? • How is the information from the monitoring process used to identify problems or improve performance?	• What prevents you or primary care providers from carrying out their role and responsibilities? • How can PCPs be better supported to carry out their responsibilities during the initial patient encounter? • Other recommendations?

The next questions are about what happens after the initial patient encounter.

	Roles/Responsibilities	Implementation	Monitoring	Barriers/Facilitators
Monitoring Patients	• What are the role and responsibilities of the PCP after the initial patient encounter? • What is the PCP's role (if any) in addressing: - treatment nonadherence? - unresponsiveness to treatment? - side effects? • What is your role in ensuring that PCPs carry out these responsibilities?	• How effective is RESPECT-Mil in supporting PCPs in monitoring and addressing problems that arise in treatment? • What has *not* been effective?	• How are PCPs monitored (if at all) with respect to their RESPECT-Mil responsibilities after the initial patient encounter? • How is the information from the monitoring process used to identify problems or improve performance?	• How can PCPs be better supported to carry out their responsibilities after the initial patient encounter (e.g., treatment nonadherence, unresponsiveness, and side effects)? • Other recommendations?

	Roles/Responsibilities	Implementation	Monitoring	Barriers/Facilitators
Coordination	• Now I'm going to ask you about the coordination of care among providers. • What is the PCP's role in coordinating care with other providers (e.g., CFs, BHCs)? • To what extent is the coordination of patient care similar to what is prescribed by RESPECT-Mil?	• How effective is RESPECT-Mil in coordinating patient care with PCPs, CFs and BHCs? • What is *not* working?	• How is coordination of care monitored? • How is information from the monitoring process used to identify problems or improve performance?	• What would facilitate better coordination of care between PCPs, CFs, and BHCs? • Other recommendations?

Closing questions:
- Given all the various roles and responsibilities discussed, what happens when there is staff turnover (e.g., permanent change of station, deployment)? Any preparations in place?
- How has RESPECT-Mil affected patient care?
- How is RESPECT-Mil similar or different from other behavioral health initiatives such as the Patient Centered Medical Home?
- In your opinion, what needs to change the most in the way that the military health system addresses the behavioral health concerns of service members?
- Ask PCC to nominate the best- and worst-performing primary care provider with respect to implementation of the RESPECT-Mil program.

Discussion Protocol for Primary Care Providers

Opening questions:
- How long have you been working with RESPECT-Mil?
- How long at this current site?
- What has been your overall experience with RESPECT-Mil?
- What's useful?
- What's not useful?

The next questions are about your activities around caring for patients with PTSD or depression.

	Roles/Responsibilities	Implementation	Monitoring	Barriers/Facilitators
Initial Patient Encounter	• What's your role (if any) in: - identifying patients with PTSD or depression? - treatment planning? - treatment referrals (to RESPECT-Mil)? - addressing treatment barriers (e.g., treatment will hurt their career; don't need treatment; meds. are addictive; side effects)? • How are these processes the same or different for PTSD vs. depression?	• You've told me what you do during the initial patient encounter; how does this fit with what is prescribed by the RESPECT-Mil program? • How effective is RESPECT-Mil in: • identifying PTSD or depression? • facilitating access to mental health treatment? • addressing treatment barriers? • In what ways is RESPECT-Mil *not* working? • In what ways is it working?	• How is your implementation of the RESPECT-Mil program monitored (if at all)? • How is the information from the monitoring process used to identify problems or improve performance?	• What prevents you from being able to carry out your role and responsibilities? • What would help you to carry out your responsibilities better during initial patient encounters? • Any other recommendations on how to improve this process?
Monitoring patients	• What is your role after the initial patient encounter? • What is your role, if any, in addressing: • treatment nonadherence? • unresponsiveness to treatment? • side effects? • How do you know what happens to patients after their initial visit with you?	• You've told me some of the things you do after the initial patient encounter; how does this fit with what is prescribed by the RESPECT-Mil program? • How effective is RESPECT-Mil in monitoring and addressing problems that arise in behavioral health treatment plans? • What has *not* been effective?	• How is your role in caring for patients after the initial visit being monitored? • How is the information from the monitoring process used to identify problems or improve performance?	• What would help you to monitor patients better after the initial encounter? • How can you be better supported to address treatment nonadherence, unresponsiveness, and side effects? • Other recommendations?

Now I'm going to ask you about the coordination of care among providers.

	Roles/Responsibilities	Implementation	Monitoring	Barriers/Facilitators
Coordination	• What is your role in coordinating care with CFs? • What information do you provide to and receive from CFs? • How is information exchanged?	• How does the coordination of care that you described fit with what is prescribed by RESPECT-Mil? • How effective is RESPECT-Mil in facilitating the coordination of care between PCPs, CFs, and BHCs? • What hasn't been effective?	• How is the coordination of care monitored? • How is information from the monitoring process used to identify problems or improve performance?	• What would facilitate better coordination of care between PCPs, CFs, and BHCs? • Other recommendations?

Closing questions:
- Given all the various roles and responsibilities discussed, what happens when there is staff turnover (e.g., permanent change of station, deployment)? Any preparations in place?
- How has RESPECT-Mil affected patient care?
- How is RESPECT-Mil similar or different from other behavioral health initiatives such as the Patient Centered Medical Home?
- In your opinion, what needs to change the most in the way that the military health system addresses the behavioral health concerns of service members?

RMIT Internal Process Discussion Protocol

This appendix presents the discussion protocol for the RMIT internal process.

Grand tour questions

- In your opinion, what is the mission or objectives of RMIT?
- How are these objectives supposed to be achieved?
- What is your role and responsibilities within RMIT?
- What factors facilitate or inhibit the functioning of RMIT?

For the next set of questions, I'm going to ask you about specific RMIT responsibilities. I'm going to ask you about what is involved with various responsibilities, who is responsible, what's working and what's not working, recommendations for improving the process, and whether any kind of monitoring is in place to track performance of these responsibilities.

Roles and responsibilities with respect to . . .	What is involved in this step?	Who is responsible for this step?		What is working and not working?	What can be improved at this step?	What kind of monitoring process (if any) is in place to track performance at this step?
		RMIT member(s)	Clinic site member(s)			
Preparing the practice settings						
Hiring/staffing						
Training providers and champions (e.g., RCFs, PCCs, BHCs, administrative assistants)						
Addressing staff turnover (e.g., permanent change of station, deployment)						
Monitoring implementation (RCFs; PCPs; BHCs; PCCs)						
Coaching calls						
Site assessment visits						
Providing feedback to installations (e.g., quarterly reports)						
Providing incentives for implementing RESPECT-Mil						

The next set of questions is about the possible role and responsibilities of others who may be involved in supporting the implementation of RESPECT-Mil.

Roles and responsibilities With respect to . . .	What is the role of "X" (if any) in supporting the implementation of RESPECT-Mil?	What is working and not working?	What can be improved?
Clinic administrators			
Installation-level command			
Regional Medical Command			

Closing questions:
- Of all of the things that RMIT does, what do you think has the most impact on sites?
- What do you think is a waste of time?
- How is RMIT doing with respect to program development and interfacing with the larger behavioral health care system?

Discussion Protocol for Stakeholder Discussions

1. Familiarity with the RESPECT-Mil
   a. How familiar are you with the RESPECT-Mil program?
   b. What are your perceptions of the RESPECT-Mil program?
2. Role of RESPECT-Mil with respondent's organization
   a. Can you give me a sense of how RESPECT-Mil fits with your organization?
   b. In what ways, if at all, does RESPECT-Mil contribute toward your organization's mission?
3. Positive and negative aspects of RESPECT-Mil
   a. What are your thoughts about whether the program is headed in the right or wrong direction?
   b. What factors may contribute to ending support for RESPECT-Mil?
   c. What factors may lead to continued support for RESPECT-Mil?
4. RESPECT-Mil compared with other initiatives
   a. To what degree is RESPECT-Mil similar to or different from other behavioral health initiatives within the military health system (e.g., Patient Centered Medical Home)?
      ◦ What does RESPECT-Mil lack compared with other initiatives?
      ◦ What does RESPECT-Mil have that other initiatives lack?
5. Improvements and recommendations
   a. In your opinion, what needs to change the most in the way the military health system addresses the behavioral health concerns of active duty service members?

Qualitative Analysis Details

Following the call, the note taker produced written notes, and the discussion facilitator checked and validated the notes. Any additions or discrepancies were discussed in order to produce a final set of notes agreed on by both the discussion facilitator and the note taker.

After completion of the discussions, we believed that it would be important to put certain quotes in the context of implementation at the particular site. For instance, some providers described a highly functional program and made suggestions about further improvement, whereas others described a program that was not functioning well and saw no room for improvement. Therefore, we examined each discussion to determine whether the respondent described RESPECT-Mil procedures that were aligned with the RESPECT-Mil program.

Discussions were rated as "partially aligned" for respondents who described limitations in the RESPECT-Mil implementation at their sites, "aligned" for those who described procedures consistent with the RESPECT-Mil manuals, and "high" for those who described innovations that appeared to go above and beyond the procedures outlined in the RESPECT-Mil manual. Specific examples were used to anchor each rating for discussions of each provider type. Two researchers rated each discussion, and any discrepancies were discussed and resolved.

Discussion notes were divided into individual quotes consisting of one or more sentences that seemed to reflect a single idea. Quotes were entered onto individual slips of paper that noted their source (identification number, type of provider, site), alignment with RESPECT-Mil, and the section of the discussion in which it appeared. These were used to provide context to the quote during the analytic process, as needed, if it was difficult to interpret the quote on its own.

These quotes were then sorted independently by two researchers according to discussions from each provider type. Each researcher independently put the quote into piles of similar content or theme, and then the two researchers met to review the piles and reach a consensus on the pile names and on the appropriate pile for each quote. Quotes that fit more than one pile were duplicated and entered into two or three piles as needed. Quotes from BHCs were completed first, resulting in 11 different piles for 107 quotes, and 4 quotes that were deemed not useful. For the other provider types (PCCs, PCPs, and RCFs), these 11 themes were used as a starting point, so that quotes could be put into piles for those themes, as well as creating additional piles that represented a new theme if necessary. Provider discussions and RMIT discussions were sorted in a similar way, but by developing a new set of themes for the RMIT discussions.

Following the pile-sort procedures, we developed an outline of the report that would cover the basic themes that emerged. Within each section, we reexamined the quotes for a particular theme across provider types. In this review, we took into account the source of the quote (individual and site), alignment with the RESPECT-Mil program, and placement within the discussion in order to appropriately understand the quote in context. We then summarized the main idea of the theme, the benefits and challenges within the theme, and the variability in opinions that we observed within the theme.

Baseline and Last Follow-Up PCL Scores

Baseline Prominent Symptoms	Among Service Members with a Follow-Up Assessment Recorded			
	Baseline		Last Follow-Up	
	Mean	Standard Deviation	Mean	Standard Deviation
Depression (*N* = 350)	15.1	3.6	9.2	6.4
PTSD (*N* = 403)	46.3	10.4	39.9	15.6
DEP+PTSD				
Depression (*N* = 375)	16.8	4.3	11.1	6.9
PTSD (*N* = 348)	57.7	12.4	46.6	18.5

Crosswalk of Recommendations and Findings

Table N.1
3CM: PCP and the Prepared Practice (Screening, Assessment, Referral, and Management)

Recommendations	Quantitative Findings	Qualitative Findings
• Routine screening is seen as a major strength of this program, but is not conducted in all settings. Implement screening in all primary care settings (including in theater, aid stations, team rooms, joint posts, special ops, U.S. Army Forces Command), but note that any screening efforts should go hand in hand with solid evidence-based program elements to handle service members who screen positive. At the same time, explore ways to streamline the process to ease the administrative burden, including the possibility of bypassing screening for those that have recently been screened and already referred to RESPECT-Mil.	• Large variability observed in screening rates, but the majority of sites screen 90 percent or more of primary care service members. • 8 percent of positive screens result in referrals that are declined. • Among service members with mild to severe clinical symptoms, a substantial proportion are documented as being lost before establishing RCF contact or at last RCF contact due to an inability to contact or engage service members.	• Almost everyone agreed that screening in primary care is important because it catches people who may have been off the radar and is a major strength of RESPECT-Mil. • But there are many challenges to be surmounted, including limited staff time, some PCP discomfort with handling behavioral health issues in primary care, and getting providers on board for screening and referral due to these two factors.
• PCPs are a critical part of the RESPECT-Mil program but are not always cooperating fully with it. Consider additional ways to increase engagement of PCPs by monitoring their individual performance and increasing their comfort level in working with behavioral issues through additional training and work with the PCC. Consider also structural or cultural changes that might facilitate the time and effort needed by PCPs to address mental health issues. • PCCs have severe constraints on their time and need to demonstrate productivity outside the RESPECT-Mil program. Consider ways to incentivize and recognize those in the champion positions so that they can devote adequate time to the program. PCCs could work more closely with PCPs who have low referral rates or discomfort with managing mental health issues in primary care.	• Large variability in referral of service members who screen positive. • Rate of accepted RESPECT-Mil referrals range from less than 2 percent to 18 percent of positive screens.	

Table N.1—Continued

Recommendations	Quantitative Findings	Qualitative Findings
• RESPECT-Mil was designed for individuals with PTSD and/or depression, but is including many service members with subthreshold symptoms as well. Since many service members with subthreshold symptoms have significant psychosocial impairment, it may be appropriate to include these service members. Consider ways the program might be adapted in light of this service member mix. • Determine the value of screening service members already enrolled in behavioral health care. Nearly half of the positive screens were documented as already being followed in behavioral health and no referral was issued. Flagging service members who are experiencing clinically significant depression and/or PTSD symptoms despite being followed in behavioral health may provide an opportunity to intervene to ensure that adequate levels of treatment are being obtained.	• Less than half of service members meet the full criteria for a probable depression or PTSD diagnosis, another quarter have mild to moderate symptoms, and more than a tenth (16 percent) have no or minimal symptoms. • 46 percent of the positive screens were recorded as already being solely followed in behavioral health.	
• Because of frequent staff turnover, the RESPECT-Mil program is constantly in flux within clinics. Consider ways to establish ongoing training and peer mentoring within the program to enable a quick start and stabilize the program over time.		• At some sites, staff turnover and training goes smoothly, but at other sites it can really disrupt RESPECT-Mil implementation.
• Command support is seen as critical for this program, but service members do not always admit to symptoms because they perceive a lack of support from their commanders. Continue and enhance command support and engagement in the program so that service members can honestly report their symptoms.		• Getting command buy-in is also seen as critical to success of the program.

Table N.2
3CM: RESPECT-Mil Care Facilitator (Support, Monitoring, and Communication)

Recommendations	Quantitative Findings	Qualitative Findings
• Overall, the RESPECT-Mil program provides a good model for addressing PTSD and depression through primary care. Processes of care in RESPECT-Mil are comparable to some civilian and VA studies, but less intensive than outlined in the RESPECT-Mil manuals and training. Consider ways to either adapt the program to reflect actual implementation (e.g., how to maximize care with fewer visits, shorter timeline) or explore strategies to increase service member engagement throughout the entire course of treatment.	• Among service members who had at least one follow-up clinical assessment recorded, some improvement was observed; 30–40 percent of patients who started out with high symptoms showed improvement during the program. However, at the last follow-up assessment, about a third still met the criteria for PTSD or depression. Rates of probable diagnosis at last follow-up assessment were even higher for service members presenting with both depression and PTSD symptoms. These outcomes are comparable with civilian or VA studies, despite the fact that RESPECT-Mil includes patients with subthreshold symptoms. However, the length of treatment is somewhat shorter in RESPECT-Mil than in the other studies.	• Overall, coordination of care was seen as functional and as improving service member care. Many see the CF role as central to the success of the program, but there was some desire to have greater transparency in performance at the CF level.
• Given lower engagement of service members in care than desired, consider ways to enhance the handoff between the PCP and the RCF, including training PCPs in describing the program and providing warm handoffs within the clinic. • Given lower engagement of service members in care than desired, consider ways to facilitate communication and engagement with service members via newer technologies for communication (such as texting and social media) and training RCFs in engagement and motivational interviewing strategies, as currently being tested in the STEPS-UP project. • Given the reluctance of some service members to seek care and the perceived discouragement of care from some commanders, train commanders on the potential impact of policies that discourage mental health care on the health of the force, and explore ways to encourage and incentivize use of mental health services among service members.	• A substantial number (38 percent) of RESPECT-Mil referred service members with mild to severe depression and/or PTSD symptoms do not establish contact with the RCF. This finding is in the middle range of several similar studies, and similar to a few (27 percent in Wells, Sherbourne, Schoenbaum, et al., 2000; 44 percent in Chaney et al., 2011). • Engagement with the RCF was somewhat lower than outlined in the RESPECT-Mil manual, with only 60 percent having a meeting within 14 days of being initially referred to the program. • Service members had an average of 2.6 RCF follow-up contacts and were enrolled in the program for a mean of 57 days. However, these rates are similar to civilian and VA studies (Dietrich et al., 2004; Fortney, Enderle, et al., 2012). • Service members' reported use or PCPs' recommended use of medications increased from 9 percent at baseline to 53 percent during subsequent RCF follow-up contacts. • Service members' reported attendance or PCPs' recommended attendance of counseling increased from 14 percent at baseline to 67 percent during subsequent RCF follow-up contacts. • Approximately 39 percent started a medication during the program, and 23 percent started counseling. These rates are somewhat lower than those found in civilian and VA studies.	• Care facilitators have some difficulty reaching service members via telephone. Some preferred face-to-face contact; others felt that service members were not motivated to begin treatment or were discouraged from getting care (concerned about the impact of medications on career or not allowed to take off work for appointments). • Decisionmaking by some PCPs included triaging more-severe cases and sending them to behavioral health rather than RESPECT-Mil; PCPs show some discomfort with treating PTSD in particular. • Discussions of the process of care primarily focused on medication management.

Table N.2—Continued

Recommendations	Quantitative Findings	Qualitative Findings

• Given constraints on communication:
  – Identify ways to provide feedback for patients (positive and negative) to PCPs who referred them into the program.
  – Consider ways to improve communication outside of the medical record system, such as colocation and cross-unit meetings focused on patient care.
  – Explore ways to integrate and streamline record management systems.
		• Several respondents discussed issues with communication and record keeping in the FIRST-STEPS system and communication in the AHLTA system. Integration of the two systems is strongly desired.

Table N.3
3CM: BHC (Informal Advice to PCPs, Review Cases with RCF, and Consultations and Facilitation of Specialty Care)

Recommendations	Quantitative Findings	Qualitative Findings
• Given the importance of the BHC role, discomfort with mental health treatment among some PCPs, and communication issues described by some, consider enhancing the BHC role, particularly in the larger sites, through changes in location, availability, and incentives. • BHCs have severe constraints on their time and the need to demonstrate productivity outside the RESPECT-Mil program. Consider ways to incentivize and recognize those in the champion positions so that they can devote adequate time to the program. • BHCs could work more closely with PCPs to increase comfort with medication management for service members with more-severe symptoms.		• The BHC role was described as being a mentor or coach to the PCPs, and there was general agreement that this was working well. • However, respondents viewed the BHC as stretched thin, with competing priorities related to regular duties and few incentives to participate.

Table N.4
Monitoring Implementation of RESPECT-Mil

Recommendations	Quantitative Findings	Qualitative Findings
• Given the challenges in central monitoring in real time, consider ways to streamline this process or to build in more routine on-site monitoring of providers. • Explore ways to monitor individual-level performance of key RESPECT-Mil staff and incentivize high performers. Use of service member–level data may enhance this effort. • Look for ways to increase buy-in to the monitoring process, and develop ways for sites to self-monitor certain aspects. This may increase ownership over and investment in the monitoring process.	• Clinic-level data for this project were made available to us by the RMIT team, indicating that they are gathering and monitoring both processes and outcomes at the clinic level. Individual-level data, however, were not available to the RMIT team prior to this project.	• Views on monitoring were very mixed. Some participants saw little in the way of monitoring, particularly among the BHCs. Participants discussed the FIRST-STEPS system as a means to structure RCF behavior, site calls, and site visits with the RMIT team; metrics returned to the sites on their performance; and natural peer review and monitoring within the program. Criticisms of each method were prominent. • The RMIT team described monitoring as one of their main functions, and acknowledged time lags in performance metrics as a problem. • Few incentives to increase performance were described.

Table N.5
RESPECT-Mil Implementation Team (Overall Impressions, Internal Processes and Functioning, and Larger System Influences)

Recommendations	Quantitative Findings	Qualitative Findings
• Retain the RMIT or a similar entity for programs that are rolled out across multiple settings to help preserve fidelity and provide direction as local adaptations are considered. • Given limited resources and uncertainties about the impact of some aspects of their activities, evaluate the relative impact of adapting current activities and different monitoring tools and consider ways to decentralize some aspects (e.g., put some responsibility for monitoring on the sites themselves). • Garner command support and buy-in, at installation and RMC levels, to facilitate program implementation.		• The RMIT team described challenges in being able to train staff and monitor sites from afar, both in terms of having too few staff for the job and in providing timely feedback to sites. • Some RMIT members raised questions about the effectiveness of some activities, such as site calls, in improving site performance. The RMIT's role in troubleshooting and working between site staff and RMCs was also seen as important.

Table N.6
Big Picture Issues: Addressing Behavioral Health Concerns of Service Members, Stigma, and Transition to PCMH

Recommendations	Quantitative Findings	Qualitative Findings
• With the addition of PCMH, RESPECT-Mil will adapt. Careful consideration is needed to determine the aspects of RESPECT-Mil that add value and can be preserved within that system. Based on this work, it appears that several aspects are thought to be important and should be preserved. • Larger system and cultural issues, beyond the health system, will be important to address in order to encourage service members to seek help when in need. These include leadership training and consideration of policies that may currently discourage mental health care. • Continued monitoring and oversight of the RESPECT-Mil program and PCMH will be necessary as these programs change and adapt over time.		• RESPECT-Mil appears to reduce stigma, but there is still reluctance among service members to seek care (e.g., many believe that getting treatment could harm their careers). • RESPECT-Mil attempts to facilitate entrance into behavioral health care, but sometimes the behavioral health system is at capacity and there are long waiting lists. Some suggested that embedding or colocating mental health assets in primary care, like in PCMH, could help. • Some respondents saw the disability system as being problematic and suggested that it rewards failure rather than success. • Some suggested a need to attend more to service members' families and support systems, who can affect whether a service member gets help or recovers. • With the addition of the PCMH program, there was mixed opinion about whether the two programs could be compatible or whether they would compete for resources. Some discussed the unique aspects of RESPECT-Mil that should be maintained within PCMH: routine screening, training on medications for PCPs, and monitoring and oversight by RMIT. • Stakeholders had some consensus on the need to reevaluate mental health initiatives since DoD has rolled out many programs related to enhancing mental health services, and now needs to assess the effectiveness of them and compare approaches to see which are the best and most cost-effective.

Abbreviations

3CM	Three Component Model
AHLTA	Armed Forces Health Longitudinal Technology Application
BHC	behavioral health champion
BHCM	behavioral health case managers
CALM	Coordinated Anxiety Learning and Management
CF	care facilitator
DCoE	Defense Centers of Excellence for Psychological Health and Traumatic Brain Injury
DEP+PTSD	depression plus PTSD prominent
DoD	Department of Defense
DSM-IV	*Diagnostic and Statistical Manual of Mental Disorders*, 4th edition
FIRST-STEPS	Fast Informative Risk and Safety Tracker and Stepped Treatment Entry and Planning System
GAO	Government Accountability Office
IBHC	internal behavioral health consultant
IDES	Integrated Disability Evaluation System
IMPACT	Improving Mood-Promoting Access to Collaborative Treatment
MEDCOM	U.S. Army Medical Command
MTF	military treatment facility
OEF	Operation Enduring Freedom
OIF	Operation Iraqi Freedom
OND	Operation New Dawn
OTSG	Office of the Surgeon General
PCC	primary care champion
PCL	Posttraumatic Stress Disorder Checklist—Civilian Version

PCMH	Patient Centered Medical Home
PCP	primary care provider
PC-PTSD	Primary Care PTSD
PDHA	Post-Deployment Health Assessment
PHQ-2	Patient Health Questionnaire-2
PHQ-9	Patient Health Questionnaire-9
PTSD	posttraumatic stress disorder
RCF	RESPECT-Mil care facilitator
RCT	randomized controlled trial
RE-AIM	Reach, Efficacy, Adoption, Implementation, Maintenance
RESPECT-D	Re-Engineering Primary Care Treatment of Depression
RESPECT-Mil	Re-Engineering Systems of Primary Care Treatment in the Military
RESPECT-PTSD	Re-Engineering Systems for the Primary Care Treatment of PTSD
RMC	Regional Medical Command
RMIT	RESPECT-Mil Implementation Team
SCL-20	Symptom Checklist–20
STEPS-UP	Stepped Enhancement of PTSD Services Using Primary Care
T-Cons	Telephone Consults
TEAM	Telemedicine Enhanced Antidepressant Management
TIDES	Translating Initiatives for Depression into Effective Solutions
VA	Department of Veterans Affairs

References

American Psychiatric Association, *Diagnostic and Statistical Manual of Mental Disorders, Fourth Edition, Text Revision, DSM-IV*, Washington, DC: American Psychiatric Association, 2000.

Archer, J., P. Bower, S. Gilbody, K. Lovell, D. Richards, L. Gask, C. Dickens, and P. Coventry, "Collaborative Care for Depression and Anxiety Problems," *Cochrane Database of Systematic Reviews*, Vol. 10, 2012, pp. 1–120.

Barry, Sheila L., and Thomas E. Oxman, *RESPECT-Mil: Care Facilitator Reference Manual*, Three Component Model, 3CM LLC-Version MIL-2.0, Dartmouth Medical School, 2008. As of January 31, 2014: http://www.pdhealth.mil/respect-mil/downloads/FAC_Final.pdf

Campbell, D. G., B. L. Felker, C. F. Liu, E. M. Yano, J. E. Kirchner, D. Chan, L. V. Rubenstein, and E. F. Chaney, "Prevalence of Depression-PTSD Comorbidity: Implications for Clinical Practice Guidelines and Primary Care-Based Interventions," *Journal of General Internal Medicine*, Vol. 22, No. 6, June 2007, pp. 711–718.

Chan, D., M. Y. Fan, and J. Unützer, "Long-Term Effectiveness of Collaborative Depression Care in Older Primary Care Patients With and Without PTSD Symptoms," *International Journal of Geriatric Psychiatry*, Vol. 26, No. 7, July 2011, pp. 758–764.

Chaney, E. F., L. V. Rubenstein, C. F. Liu, E. M. Yano, C. Bolkan, M. Lee, B. Simon, A. Lanto, B. Felker, and J. Uman, "Implementing Collaborative Care for Depression Treatment in Primary Care: A Cluster Randomized Evaluation of a Quality Improvement Practice Redesign," *Implementation Science*, Vol. 6, 2011, p. 121.

Craske, Michelle G., Murray B. Stein, Greer Sullivan, Cathy Sherbourne, Alexander Bystritsky, Raphael D. Rose, Ariel J. Lang, Stacy Welch, Laura Campbell-Sills, Daniela Golinelli, and P. Roy-Byrne, "Disorder-Specific Impact of Coordinated Anxiety Learning and Management Treatment for Anxiety Disorders in Primary Care," *Archives of General Psychiatry*, Vol. 68, No. 4, 2011, pp. 378–388.

Curran, G. M., C. R. Thrush, J. L. Smith, R. R. Owen, M. Ritchie, and D. Chadwick, "Implementing Research Findings into Practice Using Clinical Opinion Leaders: Barriers and Lessons Learned," *Joint Commission Journal on Quality and Patient Safety*, Vol. 31, 2005, pp. 700–707.

Department of Defense Task Force on Mental Health, *An Achievable Vision: Report of the Department of Defense Task Force on Mental Health*, Falls Church, VA: Defense Health Board, 2007.

Deployment Health Clinical Center, *RESPECT-Mil*, newsletter, Summer 2012. As of January 31, 2014: http://www.pdhealth.mil/downloads/Mil_Newsletter%20Summer%202012.pdf

Derogatis, L. R., R. S. Lipman, and L. Covi, "SCL-90: An Outpatient Psychiatric Rating Scale—Preliminary Report," *Psychopharmacology Bulletin*, Vol. 9, No. 1, January 1973, pp. 13–28.

Dietrich, Allen J., Thomas E. Oxman, John W. Williams Jr., Herbert C. Schulberg, Martha L. Bruce, Pamela W. Lee, Sheila Barry, Patrick J. Raue, Jean J. Lefever, and Moonseong Heo, "Re-Engineering Systems for the Treatment of Depression in Primary Care: Cluster Randomised Controlled Trial," *British Medical Journal*, Vol. 329, No. 7,466, 2004, p. 602.

Engel, Charles C., Thomas Oxman, Christopher Yamamoto, Darin Gould, Sheila Barry, Patrice Stewart, Kurt Kroenke, John W. Williams, and Allen J. Dietrich, "RESPECT-Mil—Feasibility of a Systems-Level Collaborative Care Approach to Depression and Post-Traumatic Stress Disorder in Military Primary Care," *Military Medicine*, Vol. 173, No. 10, 2008, pp. 935–940.

Felker, Bradford L., Edmund Chaney, Lisa V. Rubenstein, Laura M. Bonner, Elizabeth M. Yano, Louise E. Parker, Linda L. M. Worley, Scott E. Sherman, and Scott Ober, "Developing Effective Collaboration Between Primary Care and Mental Health Providers," *Primary Care Companion to the Journal of Clinical Psychiatry*, Vol. 8, No. 1, 2006, pp. 12–16.

First, Michael B., Robert L. Spitzer, Miriam Gibbon, and Janet B. W. Williams, *Structured Clinical Interview for DSM-IV Axis I Disorders, Clinician Version (SCID-CV)*, Washington, DC: American Psychiatric Association, 1997.

Fortney, John, Mark Enderle, Skye McDougall, Jeff Clothier, Jay Otero, Lisa Altman, and Geoff Curran, "Implementation Outcomes of Evidence-Based Quality Improvement for Depression in VA Community Based Outpatient Clinics," *Implementation Science*, Vol. 7, 2012, p. 30.

Fortney, John C., Jeffrey M. Pyne, Mark J. Edlund, David K. Williams, Dean E. Robinson, Dinesh Mittal, and Kathy L. Henderson, "A Randomized Trial of Telemedicine-Based Collaborative Care for Depression," *Journal of General Internal Medicine*, Vol. 22, No. 8, 2007, pp. 1086–1093.

Fortney, John C., Jeffrey M. Pyne, Jeff L. Smith, Geoffrey M. Curran, Jay M. Otero, Mark A. Enderle, and Skye McDougall, "Steps for Implementing Collaborative Care Programs for Depression," *Health Population Management*, Vol. 12, No. 2, 2009, pp. 69–79.

Frayne, Susan M., Victor Y. Chiu, Samina Iqbal, Eric A. Berg, Kaajal J. Laungani, and Joanne Pavao, "Medical Care Needs of Returning Veterans with PTSD: Their Other Burden," *Journal of General Internal Medicine*, Vol. 26, No. 1, 2011, pp. 33–39.

GAO—*See* U.S. Government Accountability Office.

Gilbody, Simon, Peter Bower, Janine Fletcher, David Richards, and Alex J. Sutton, "Collaborative Care for Depression: A Cumulative Meta-Analysis and Review of Longer-Term Outcomes," *Archives of Internal Medicine*, Vol. 166, No. 21, 2006, pp. 2314–2321.

Glasgow, Russell E., Thomas M. Vogt, and Shawn M. Boles, "Evaluating the Public Health Impact of Health Promotion Interventions: The RE-AIM Framework," *American Journal of Public Health*, Vol. 89, No. 9, 1999, pp. 1322–1327.

Grubaugh, Anouk L., Kathryn M. Magruder, Angela E. Waldrop, Jon D. Elhai, Rebecca G. Knapp, and B. Christopher Frueh, "Subthreshold PTSD in Primary Care: Prevalence, Psychiatric Disorders, Healthcare Use, and Functional Status," *The Journal of Nervous and Mental Disease*, Vol. 193, No. 10, 2005, pp. 658–664.

Hedrick, Susan C., Edmund F. Chaney, Bradford Felker, Chuan-Fen Liu, Nicole Hasenberg, Patrick Heagerty, Jan Buchanan, Rocco Bagala, Diane Greenberg, Grady Paden, Stephan D. Fihn, and Wayne Katon, "Effectiveness of Collaborative Care Depression Treatment in Veterans' Affairs Primary Care," *Journal of General Internal Medicine*, Vol. 18, No. 1, 2003, pp. 9–16.

Hegel, Mark T., Jürgen Unützer, Lingqi Tang, Patricia A. Areán, Wayne Katon, Polly Hitchcock Noël, John W. Williams Jr., and Elizabeth H. B. Lin, "Impact of Comorbid Panic and Posttraumatic Stress Disorder on Outcomes of Collaborative Care for Late-Life Depression in Primary Care," *American Journal of Geriatric Psychiatry*, Vol. 13, No. 1, 2005, pp. 48–58.

Hoge, Charles W., Jennifer L. Auchterlonie, and Charles S. Milliken, "Mental Health Problems, Use of Mental Health Services, and Attrition from Military Service After Returning from Deployment to Iraq or Afghanistan," *JAMA: The Journal of the American Medical Association*, Vol. 295, No. 9, 2006, pp. 1023–1032.

Independent Review Group on Rehabilitative Care and Administrative Processes at Walter Reed Army Medical Center and National Naval Medical Center, *Rebuilding the Trust: Report on Rehabilitative Care and Administrative Processes at Walter Reed Army Medical Center and National Naval Medical Center*, Arlington, VA: Independent Review Group, 2007.

Institute of Medicine, *Treatment for Posttraumatic Stress Disorder in Military and Veteran Populations: Initial Assessment*, Washington, DC: The National Academies Press, 2012. As of August 23, 2013: http://www.nap.edu/openbook.php?record_id=13364

———, *Treatment for Posttraumatic Stress Disorder in Military and Veteran Populations: Final Assessment*, Washington, DC: The National Academies Press, 2014.

Judd, Lewis L., Martin P. Paulus, Kenneth B. Wells, and Mark H. Rapaport, "Socioeconomic Burden of Subsyndromal Depressive Symptoms and Major Depression in a Sample of the General Population," *American Journal of Psychiatry*, Vol. 153, No. 11, 1996, pp. 1411–1417.

Kroenke, Kurt, and Robert L. Spitzer, "The PHQ-9: A New Depression Diagnostic and Severity Measure," *Psychiatric Annals*, Vol. 32, No. 9, 2002, pp. 1–7.

Kroenke, Kurt, Robert L. Spitzer, and Janet B. W. Williams, "The PHQ-9: Validity of a Brief Depression Severity Measure," *Journal of General Internal Medicine*, Vol. 16, No. 9, 2001, pp. 606–613.

———, "The Patient Health Questionnaire-2: Validity of a Two-Item Depression Screener," *Medical Care*, Vol. 41, No. 11, 2003, pp. 1284–1292.

Liu, Chuan-Fen, John Fortney, Susan Vivell, Karen Vollen, William N. Raney, Barbara Revay, Maurilio Garcia-Maldonado, Jeffrey Pyne, Lisa V. Rubenstein, and Edmund Chaney, "Time Allocation and Caseload Capacity in Telephone Depression Care Management-Page 4," *American Journal of Managed Care*, Vol. 13, 2007, pp. 652–660.

Meyer, Christian, Sabina Ulbricht, Beatrice Gross, Lissy Kästel, Sabine Wittrien, Gudrun Klein, Britta A Skoeries, Hans-Jürgen Rumpf, and Ulrich John, "Adoption, Reach and Effectiveness of Computer-Based, Practitioner Delivered and Combined Smoking Interventions in General Medical Practices: A Three-Arm Cluster Randomized Trial," *Drug and Alcohol Dependence*, Vol. 121, No. 1, 2012, pp. 124–132.

Monson, Candice M., Paula P. Schnurr, Patricia A. Resick, Matthew J. Friedman, Yinong Young-Xu, and Susan P. Stevens, "Cognitive Processing Therapy for Veterans with Military-Related Posttraumatic Stress Disorder," *Journal of Consulting and Clinical Psychology*, Vol. 74, No. 5, 2006, p. 898.

National Committee for Quality Assurance, *Standards and Guidelines for NCQA's Patient-Centered Medical Home (PCMH)*, Washington, DC: National Committee for Quality Assurance, 2011.

O'Connor, Elizabeth A., Evelyn P. Whitlock, Tracy L. Beil, and Bradley N. Gaynes, "Screening for Depression in Adult Patients in Primary Care Settings: A Systematic Evidence Review," *Annals of Internal Medicine*, Vol. 151, No. 11, 2009, pp. 793–803.

Oxman, Thomas E., *RESPECT-Mil Behavioral Health Specialist Manual*, Three Component Model, 3CM LLC-Version MIL-2.0, Dartmouth Medical School, 2008. As of January 31, 2014: http://www.pdhealth.mil/respect-mil/downloads/BH_Final.pdf

Oxman, Thomas E., Herbert C. Schulberg, Rebecca L. Greenberg, Allen J. Dietrich, John W. Williams Jr., Paul A. Nutting, and Martha L. Bruce, "A Fidelity Measure for Integrated Management of Depression in Primary Care," *Medical Care*, Vol. 44, No. 11, 2006, pp. 1030–1037.

President's Commission on Care for America's Returning Wounded Warriors, *Serve, Support, Simplify: Report of the President's Commission on Care for America's Returning Wounded Warriors*, Washington, DC, 2007.

Prins, Annabel, Paige Ouimette, Rachel Kimerling, Rebecca P. Cameron, Daniela S. Hugelshofer, Jennifer Shaw-Hegwer, Ann Thrailkill, Fred D. Gusman, and Javaid I. Sheikh, "The Primary Care PTSD Screen (PC-PTSD): Development and Operating Characteristics," *Primary Care Psychiatry*, Vol. 9, No. 1, 2003, pp. 9–14.

Radloff, Lenore Sawyer, "The CES-D Scale a Self-Report Depression Scale for Research in the General Population," *Applied Psychological Measurement*, Vol. 1, No. 3, 1977, pp. 385–401.

Rittenhouse, Diane R., and Stephen M. Shortell, "The Patient-Centered Medical Home," *JAMA: The Journal of the American Medical Association*, Vol. 301, No. 19, 2009, pp. 2038–2040.

Rogers, Erin, Senaida Fernandez, Colleen Gillespie, David Smelson, Hildi J. Hagedorn, Brian Elbel, David Kalman, Alfredo Axtmayer, Karishma Kurowski, and Scott E Sherman, "Telephone Care Coordination for Smokers in VA Mental Health Clinics: Protocol for a Hybrid Type-2 Effectiveness-Implementation Trial," *Addiction Science & Clinical Practice*, Vol. 8, No. 1, 2013, p. 7.

Rubenstein, L. V., E. Chaney, and J. Smith, "Improving Treatment for Depression in Primary Care," *QUERI Quarterly*, Vol. 6, 2004, pp. 1, 4.

Ryan, Gery W., Stefanie A. Stern, Lara Hilton, Joan S. Tucker, David P. Kennedy, Daniela Golinelli, and Suzanne L. Wenzel, "When, Where, Why and with Whom Homeless Women Engage in Risky Sexual Behaviors: A Framework for Understanding Complex and Varied Decision-Making Processes," *Sex Roles*, Vol. 61, Nos. 7–8, 2009, pp. 536–553.

Schell, Terry L., and Grant N. Marshall, "Survey of Individuals Previously Deployed for OEF/OIF," in *Invisible Wounds of War: Psychological and Cognitive Injuries, Their Consequences, and Services to Assist Recovery*, Terri L. Tanielian and Lisa H. Jaycox, eds., pp. 87–115, Santa Monica, CA: RAND Corporation, MG-720-CCF, 2008. As of September 10, 2013:
http://www.rand.org/pubs/monographs/MG720.html

Schnurr, Paula P., Matthew J. Friedman, David W. Foy, M. Tracie Shea, Frank Y. Hsieh, Philip W. Lavori, Shirley M. Glynn, Melissa Wattenberg, and Nancy C. Bernardy, "Randomized Trial of Trauma-Focused Group Therapy for Posttraumatic Stress Disorder: Results from a Department of Veterans Affairs Cooperative Study," *Archives of General Psychiatry*, Vol. 60, No. 5, 2003, p. 481.

Schnurr, Paula P., Matthew J. Friedman, Thomas E. Oxman, Allen J. Dietrich, Mark W. Smith, Brian Shiner, Elizabeth Forshay, Jiang Gui, and Veronica Thurston, "RESPECT-PTSD: Re-Engineering Systems for the Primary Care Treatment of PTSD, a Randomized Controlled Trial," *Journal of General Internal Medicine*, Vol. 28, No. 1, January 2013, pp. 32–40.

Smith, Jeffrey, John Williams, Richard Owen, Lisa Rubenstein, and Edmund Chaney, "Developing a National Dissemination Plan for Collaborative Care for Depression: Queri Series," *Implementation Science*, Vol. 3, No. 1, 2008, p. 59.

Tai-Seale, M., M. E. Kunik, A. Shepherd, J. Kirchner, and A. Gottumukkala, "A Case Study of Early Experience with Implementation of Collaborative Care in the Veterans Health Administration," *Population Health Management*, Vol. 13, No. 6, 2010, pp. 331–337.

Task Force on Returning Global War on Terror Heroes, task force report to the President, 2007. As of August 12, 2014:
http://www.va.gov/op3/docs/GWOTTaskforce/GWOT_TF_Report_042407.pdf

Thota, Anilkrishna B., Theresa Ann Sipe, Guthrie J. Byard, Carlos S. Zometa, Robert A. Hahn, Lela R. McKnight-Eily, Daniel P. Chapman, Ana F. Abraido-Lanza, Jane L. Pearson, Clinton W. Anderson, Alan J. Gelenberg, Kevin D. Hennessy, Farifteh F. Duffy, Mary E. Vernon-Smiley, Donald E. Nease Jr., and Samantha P. Williams, "Collaborative Care to Improve the Management of Depressive Disorders: A Community Guide Systematic Review and Meta-Analysis," *American Journal of Preventive Medicine*, Vol. 42, No. 5, May, 2012, pp. 525–538.

Tricare Management Activity, *Military Health System Patient Centered Medical Home Guide*, 2011. As of August 7, 2014:
http://www.tricare.mil/tma/ocmo/download/MHSPCMHGuide.pdf

Unützer, J., W. Katon, C. M. Callahan, J. W. Williams Jr., E Hunkeler, L. Harpole, M. Hoffing, D. P. Richard, N. Hitchcock, E. H. B. Lin, P. A. Arean, M. T. Hegel, L. Tang, T. R. Belin, S. Oishi, and C. Langston, "Collaborative Care Management of Late-Life Depression in the Primary Care Setting: A Randomized Controlled Trial," *JAMA: The Journal of the American Medical Association*, Vol. 288, No. 22, 2002, pp. 2836–2845.

U.S. Army Medical Command, "Operation Order 07-34: Re-Engineering Systems of the Primary Care Treatment (of Depression and PTSD) in the Military—RESPECT-Mil," 2007. As of July 11, 2014:
http://www.pdhealth.mil/downloads/OPORD_07-34_RESPECT-MIL.pdf

———, "Operation Order 10-25, Expansion of the Re-engineering Systems of the Primary Care Treatment of Depression and PTSD in the Military – (RESPECT-Mil) program," 2010. As of July 11, 2014:
http://www.pdhealth.mil/downloads/MEDCOM_OPORD_10-25_Expansion_Re-engineering_Systems_%205_Feb_10.pdf

U.S. Department of Veterans Affairs, National Center for PTSD, "Using the PTSD Checklist (PCL)," 2012. As of July 11, 2014:
http://www.ptsd.va.gov/professional/pages/assessments/assessment-pdf/pcl-handout.pdf

U.S. Government Accountability Office, *VA Mental Health: Number of Veterans Receiving Care, Barriers Faced, and Efforts to Increase Access*, Washington, DC: Government Accountability Office, 2011.

Warner, Christopher H., George N. Appenzeller, Thomas Grieger, Slava Belenkiy, Jill Breitbach, Jessica Parker, Carolynn M. Warner, and Charles Hoge, "Importance of Anonymity to Encourage Honest Reporting in Mental Health Screening After Combat Deployment," *Archives of General Psychiatry*, Vol. 68, No. 10, 2011, p. 1065.

Weathers, F., B. Litz, D. Herman, J. Huska, and T. Keane, "The PTSD Checklist (PCL): Reliability, Validity, and Diagnostic Utility," paper presented at the Annual Convention of the International Society for Traumatic Stress Studies, San Antonio, TX, October 1993.

Weinick, Robin M., Ellen Burke Beckjord, Carrie M. Farmer, Laurie T. Martin, Emily M. Gillen, Joie Acosta, Michael P. Fisher, Jeffrey Garnett, Gabriella C. Gonzalez, Todd C. Helmus, Lisa H. Jaycox, Kerry Reynolds, Nicholas Salcedo, and Deborah M. Scharf, *Programs Addressing Psychological Health and Traumatic Brain Injury Among U.S. Military Servicemembers and Their Families*, Santa Monica, CA.: RAND Corporation, TR-950-OSD, 2011. As of December 5, 2013:
http://www.rand.org/pubs/technical_reports/TR950

Wells, Kenneth B., Cathy Sherbourne, Naihua Duan, Jürgen Unützer, Jeanne Miranda, Michael Schoenbaum, Susan L. Ettner, Lisa S. Meredith, and Lisa Rubenstein, "Quality Improvement for Depression in Primary Care: Do Patients with Subthreshold Depression Benefit in the Long Run?" *American Journal of Psychiatry*, Vol. 162, No. 6, 2005, pp. 1149–1157.

Wells, Kenneth B., Cathy Sherbourne, Michael Schoenbaum, Naihua Duan, Lisa Meredith, Jürgen Unützer, Jeanne Miranda, Maureen F. Carney, and Lisa V. Rubenstein, "Impact of Disseminating Quality Improvement Programs for Depression in Managed Primary Care," *JAMA: The Journal of the American Medical Association*, Vol. 283, No. 2, 2000, pp. 212–220.

Zatzick, Douglas, Peter Roy-Byrne, Joan Russo, Frederick Rivara, RoseAnne Droesch, Amy Wagner, Chris Dunn, Gregory Jurkovich, Edwina Uehara, and Wayne Katon, "A Randomized Effectiveness Trial of Stepped Collaborative Care for Acutely Injured Trauma Survivors," *Archives of General Psychiatry*, Vol. 61, No. 5, 2004, pp. 498–506.